D1563040

Divorce
in Michigan

The Legal Process,
Your Rights, and What to Expect

John F. Schaefer, Esq.

Addicus Books
Omaha, Nebraska

An Addicus Nonfiction Book

ISBN 978-1-940495-29-3

Typography Jack Kusler

This book is not intended to serve as a substitute for an attorney. Nor is it the author's intent to give legal advice contrary to that of an attorney.

Library of Congress Cataloging-in-Publication Data

Schaefer, John F., (Lawyer), author.
 Divorce in Michigan : the legal process, your rights, and what to expect / John F. Schaefer, Esq.
 pages cm
 Includes index.
 ISBN 978-1-940495-29-3 (alk. paper)
 1. Divorce—Law and legislation—Michigan. I. Title.
 KFM4300.S33 2015
 346.77401'66—dc23
 2015029377

Addicus Books, Inc.
P.O. Box 45327
Omaha, Nebraska 68145
www.AddicusBooks.com
Printed in the United States of America
10 9 8 7 6 5 4 3 2 1

ii

To the many wonderful clients whom
I have represented over the past forty years.
It has, indeed, been a privilege and a pleasure.

Contents

Acknowledgments

I owe much to the attorneys and staff of The Law Firm of John F. Schaefer, especially Joan Maggard, my personal secretary and office manager, and my associate, Colleen Johnson, who did much of the heavy lifting to make this book possible. I would also like to acknowledge Rod Colvin, the publisher, and his team from Addicus Books for their encouragement and patience.

John F. Schaefer, Esq.

Introduction

I recognize that most people seeking a consultation about matrimonial matters have had little experience interacting with attorneys. Our firm is committed to attentively providing our potential clients with peace of mind by thoroughly addressing all of their questions and concerns while providing them the highest-quality professional advice and services available. I firmly believe that matrimonial law matters can be resolved in a private, dignified, and amicable manner that preserves the integrity of the parties and protects the well-being of the children.

Consulting with a matrimonial law attorney does not necessarily mean that a divorce is imminent or inevitable. Many clients seek my advice to facilitate reconciliation or simply to understand their rights.

The goal of any matrimonial lawyer should be to restore order and security to family life from what may feel like chaos and confusion. I am committed that every person who walks through my door leaves with a thorough understanding of the entire divorce process, including answers to all questions about the legal process, matters pertaining to minor children, property division, child support, spousal support, health care issues, tax issues, and attorneys fees.

The purpose of this book is not to supplant the importance of the attorney's role in these matters, but rather it is to help the uninitiated layperson to better grasp the process of divorce and related topics, and to understand some of the problems and their solutions.

When it comes to protecting a client's financial security, our financial acumen and business experience is unparalleled. In every case, we develop a detailed analysis of assets and liabilities, income and cash flow, and expenses and lifestyle. Impeccable thoroughness and accuracy are the cornerstones of our work. The reader needs to understand the importance of selecting such a champion who, through his or her knowledge, strength, and compassion, will be your partner in revitalizing your life and planning for your future.

1

Understanding the Divorce Process

At a time when your life can feel like it's in utter chaos, sometimes the smallest bit of predictability can bring a sense of comfort. The outcome of many aspects of your divorce may be unknown, increasing your fear and anxiety. But there is one part of your divorce that does have some measure of predictability and that is the divorce process itself.

Most divorces proceed in a step-by-step manner. Despite the uniqueness of your divorce, you can generally count on one phase of your divorce following the next. Sometimes just realizing you are completing stages and moving forward with your divorce can reassure you that it won't go on forever.

Develop a basic understanding of the divorce process. This will lower your anxiety when your attorney starts talking about "depositions" or "going to trial," and you feel your heart start pounding in fear. It can reduce your frustration about the length of the process because you understand why each step is needed. It will support you to begin preparing for what comes next.

Most importantly, understanding the divorce process will make your experience of the entire divorce easier. Who wouldn't prefer that?

1.1 What is my first step in seeking a divorce?

Find a law firm that handles divorces as a regular part of its law practice. The best recommendations come from people who have knowledge of a lawyer's experience and reputation.

Even if you are not ready to file for divorce, call to schedule an appointment right away to obtain information about protecting yourself and your children. Even if you are not planning to file for divorce, your spouse might be. Ask what documents you should take to your initial consultation. Make a list of your questions to bring to your first meeting. Start making plans for how you will pay your attorney to begin work on your case.

1.2 Must I have an attorney to get a divorce in Michigan?

You are not required to have an attorney to obtain a divorce in Michigan. However, if your case involves children, alimony, significant property, or debts, you should avoid proceeding on your own.

If your divorce does not involve any of these issues, contact the Legal Aid Clinic at a law school near you or your local Bar Association to request documents and instructions that are helpful in the simplest of cases. The court clerk or staff cannot provide legal advice and will not assist you other than to direct you to the appropriate court forms. A person who proceeds in a legal matter without a lawyer is referred to as being *pro se,* on one's own.

If you are considering proceeding without an attorney, at a minimum have an initial consultation with an attorney to discuss your rights and duties under the law. You may have certain rights or obligations of which you are unaware. Meeting with a lawyer can help you decide whether to proceed on your own.

1.3 What other steps are taken during the divorce process?

The divorce process in Michigan typically involves the steps listed below.

- Obtain a referral for a lawyer.
- Schedule an appointment with an attorney.
- Prepare questions and gather needed documents for initial consultation.
- Meet for initial consultation with attorney.
- Pay retainer to attorney and sign retainer agreement.

- Provide requested information and documents to your attorney.
- Take other actions as advised by attorney, such as opening or closing financial accounts.
- Attorney prepares complaint for divorce and affidavits for temporary matters for your review and signature.
- Attorney files complaint with clerk of the court. Attorney obtains *ex parte* restraining orders if appropriate. Attorney obtains hearing date for temporary matters.
- Mandatory sixty-day waiting period begins when filing the complaint.
- Negotiations begin regarding terms of temporary order on matters such as custody, support, and temporary possession of the family home. Attorneys prepare financial affidavits and child-support guidelines for temporary hearing.
- Parties reach agreement on temporary order.

OR

- Parties file motions relative to temporary matters.
- Temporary order is prepared by one attorney, approved as to form by other attorney, and submitted to the judge for signature.
- If there are minor children, parties may be required to attend a parent education class, depending on the county.
- Both sides conduct discovery to obtain information regarding all relevant facts. Obtain valuations of all assets, including expert opinions if needed.
- Ask your attorney for a litigation budget to help you anticipate and prepare for the overall cost of litigation.
- Confer with attorney to review facts, identify issues, assess strengths and weaknesses of case, review strategy, and develop proposal for settlement.
- Spouses, with support of attorneys, attempt to reach agreement through written proposals, mediation, settlement conferences, or other negotiation.

- Parties reach agreement on all issues.
- Attorney prepares judgment for divorce and court orders for the division of retirement plans for approval by spouses and attorneys.

OR

- Attorneys and parties prepare for trial and court sets a firm trial date.
- Trial preparations proceed including preparation of witnesses, trial exhibits, legal research on contested issues, pretrial motions, trial brief, preparation of direct and cross-examination of witnesses, preparation of opening statement, subpoena of witnesses, closing argument, and suggestions to the court.
- Meet with attorney for final trial preparation.
- Go to trial.
- Judge makes decision, which could take several months.
- Attorney prepares judgment.
- Other attorney approves it as to form.
- Judgment submitted to judge for signature.
- Judge signs decree of dissolution. Make payments and sign documents (deeds or titles) pursuant to judgment.
- Submit to the court documents required to divide retirement accounts and ensure the payment of child support.
- Pay any remaining balance due on attorney's fees.

1.4　Is Michigan a *no-fault* state, or do I need grounds for a divorce?

Michigan, like most states, is a *no-fault* divorce state. This means that neither you nor your spouse is required to prove that the other is "at fault" in order to be granted a divorce. Factors such as infidelity, cruelty, or abandonment are not necessary to receive a divorce in Michigan. Rather, it is necessary to prove that "there has been a breakdown of the marriage relationship to the extent that the objects of matrimony have been destroyed and there remains no reasonable likelihood the marriage can be preserved" to have it dissolved.

At the conclusion of the matter, the judge will take testimony from the party who filed confirming there has been a breakdown of the marriage. Typically, judges do not ask substantive questions as to the reasons for the breakdown of the marriage; they simply want to confirm there has been a breakdown of the marriage relationship.

1.5 How will a judge view my infidelity or my spouse's infidelity?

In a no-fault divorce state, there will rarely be testimony or evidence introduced about either spouse's infidelity. However, the judge will hear testimony regarding an extramarital affair if custody is an issue and your child was exposed to the affair.

In Michigan, a judge may consider infidelity in determining an award of alimony and in the division of property. For example, rather than dividing marital property 50/50, a judge may award a smaller percentage of the marital estate to the party who has been unfaithful.

1.6 Do I have to get divorced in the same state I married in?

No. Regardless of where you were married, you may seek a divorce in Michigan if the jurisdictional requirements of residency are met. The jurisdictional requirements are discussed in the following question.

1.7 How long must I have lived in Michigan to get a divorce in the state?

Either you or your spouse must have been a resident of Michigan for 180 days immediately preceding the filing of the complaint for divorce to meet the residency requirement for a divorce in Michigan.

If neither party meets the residency requirement, other legal options are available for your protection. If you do not meet the 180-day residency requirement, talk to your attorney about options such as a legal separation, a petition for a custody-and-support order, or a protection order.

1.8   My spouse has told me she will never "give" me a divorce. Can I get one in Michigan anyway?

Yes. Michigan does not require that your spouse agree to a divorce. If your spouse threatens to not "give" you a divorce, know that in Michigan this is likely to be an idle threat without any basis in the law.

Under Michigan law, to obtain a divorce you must be able to prove that "there has been a breakdown of the marriage relationship to the extent that the objects of matrimony have been destroyed and there remains no reasonable likelihood the marriage can be preserved." This is legal terminology meaning that one sees no possibility of reconciliation between you and your spouse. In short, it is not necessary to have your spouse agree to the divorce or to allege the specific difficulties that arose during the marriage to obtain a divorce in Michigan. Rather, it is a subjective test.

1.9   Can I divorce my spouse in Michigan if he or she lives in another state?

Provided you have met the residency requirements for living in Michigan for 180 days prior to filing the complaint for divorce, you can file for divorce here even if your spouse lives in another state. Your residency gives the State of Michigan subject matter jurisdiction.

Discuss with your attorney the facts that will need to be proven and the steps necessary to give your spouse proper notice to ensure that the court will have jurisdiction over your spouse, called *personal jurisdiction*. Your attorney can counsel you on whether it is possible to proceed with the divorce.

1.10   Can I get a divorce even if I don't know where my spouse is currently living?

Michigan law allows you to proceed with a divorce even if you do not know the current address of your spouse. First, take action to attempt to locate your spouse. Contact family members, friends, former coworkers, or anyone else who might know your spouse's whereabouts. Utilize resources on the Internet that are designed to help locate people.

Let your attorney know of the efforts you have made to attempt to find your spouse. Inform your lawyer of your spouse's last known address, as well as any work address or other address where this person may be found. Once your attorney attempts to give notice to your spouse without success, it is possible to ask the court to proceed with the divorce by giving notice through publication in a newspaper. Although your divorce may be granted following service of notice by publication in a newspaper, you may not be able to get other court orders such as those for child support or alimony without giving personal notice to your spouse. Talk to your attorney about your options and rights if you don't know where your spouse is living.

1.11 I just moved to a different county within the state of Michigan. Do I have to file in the county where my spouse lives?

You may file your divorce complaint in the county where you reside, so long as you have resided there for ten days prior to the filing of a complaint. You may also file in the county where your spouse resides.

1.12 I immigrated to Michigan. Will my immigration status stop me from getting a divorce?

If you meet the residency requirements for divorce in Michigan, you can get a divorce here notwithstanding your immigration status. Talk to your immigration lawyer about the likelihood of a divorce leading to immigration challenges.

If you are a victim of domestic violence, tell your lawyer. You may be eligible for a change in your immigration status under the federal *Violence Against Women Act.*

1.13 I want to get divorced in my Indian tribal court. What do I need to know?

Each tribal court has its own laws governing divorce. Requirements for residency, grounds for divorce, and the laws regarding property, alimony, and children can vary substantially from state law. Some tribes have very different laws governing the grounds for your divorce, removal of children from the home, and cohabitation. However, a tribal member may file for divorce in a State of Michigan court. Contact an attorney who is knowledgeable about the law in your tribal court for legal

7

advice on pursuing a divorce in your tribal court or on the requirements for recording a divorce obtained in state court with the clerk of the tribal court. Tribal court orders are given full faith and credit in the Michigan courts.

1.14   Is there a waiting period for a divorce in Michigan?
Yes. Michigan has a mandatory sixty-day waiting period in cases without minor children and a six-month waiting period in cases with minor children. The waiting period begins on the day that the complaint for divorce is filed. The court may waive the six-month waiting period in a case with minor children upon a showing of extenuating circumstances that require shortening the waiting period; however, the sixty-day waiting period may not be waived.

1.15   What is a *divorce complaint*?
A *divorce complaint* is a document signed by the person filing for divorce (the *plaintiff*) and filed with the clerk of the court to initiate the divorce process. Formerly referred to as a *petition,* the complaint will set forth in very general terms what the plaintiff is asking the court to order.

A *summons* is always filed with a divorce complaint. The summons is a document that provides instructions to the person filing as to how to serve the complaint on the *defendant* (the person not filing). It also provides instructions to the defendant as to when and how he or she must respond to the complaint. The summons also contains a *proof of service,* which is filed with the court proving that the defendant has in fact been served with a copy of the complaint. *See* the sample *Complaint for Divorce including Ex parte Orders* in the Appendix.

1.16   My spouse said she filed for divorce last week, but my lawyer says there's nothing on file at the courthouse. What does it mean to *file for divorce*?
When lawyers use the term *filing* they are ordinarily referring to filing a legal document at the courthouse, such as delivering a complaint for divorce to the clerk of the court. Sometimes a person who has hired a lawyer to begin a divorce action uses the phrase "I've filed for divorce," although no pa-

pers have yet been taken to the courthouse to start the legal process.

1.17   If we both want a divorce, does it matter who files?

No. In the eyes of the court, the plaintiff (the party who files the complaint initiating the divorce process) and the defendant (the other spouse) are not seen differently by virtue of which party filed. The court, as a neutral decision maker, will not give preference to either party. Both parties will be given adequate notice and each will have a chance to be heard and present argument.

1.18   Are there advantages to filing first?

It depends. Discuss with your attorney whether there are any advantages to your filing first. Your attorney may advise you to file first or to wait until your spouse files, depending upon the overall strategy for your case and your circumstances. For example, if there is a concern that your spouse will begin to transfer assets upon learning about your plans for divorce, your attorney might advise you to seek a temporary restraining order to protect you against such an action, without giving prior notice to your spouse. Under those circumstances, it would be beneficial to file first. However, if you are separated from your spouse but have a beneficial temporary arrangement, your attorney may counsel you to wait for your spouse to file. In a trial it may be advantageous to be first to make an opening statement.

Allow your attorney to support you in making the decision about whether and when to initiate the legal process by filing a *complaint for divorce.*

1.19   Can I stop the newspaper from publishing notice of the filing or granting of my divorce?

Documents filed with the court, such as a divorce complaint or a final decree, are matters of public record. Newspapers have a right to access this information, and many newspapers publish this information as a matter of routine.

In some cases, a divorce file may be kept private, referred to as being *sealed* or *under seal* if the court orders it. An example of a request for suppression of a case might involve a matter of particular sensitivity, notoriety, or the necessity to protect parties or their children.

1.20 Is there a way to avoid embarrassing my spouse and not have a sheriff process server serve him or her with the divorce papers at his or her workplace?

Talk to your lawyer about the option of having your spouse sign the *acknowledgment of service* on the summons, thereby accepting service of the complaint without being formally served by a process server. The signing and filing of the acknowledgment of service with the court can eliminate the need to have your spouse served by sheriff process server. A sample *Letter to Spouse* may be found on the next page.

1.21 Should I sign the acknowledgment of service even if I don't agree with what my spouse has written in the complaint for divorce?

Signing the acknowledgment of service on the summons does not mean that you agree with anything your spouse has stated in the divorce complaint or anything that your spouse is asking for in the divorce.

Signing the acknowledgment of service only substitutes for having the process server personally hand you the documents. You do not waive the right to object to anything your spouse has stated in the complaint for divorce.

Follow your attorney's advice on whether and when to sign an acknowledgment of service.

1.22 Why should I contact an attorney right away if I have received divorce papers?

If your spouse has filed for divorce, it is important that you obtain legal advice as soon as possible. Even if you and your spouse are getting along, having independent legal counsel can help you make decisions now that could affect your divorce later.

After your spouse has filed for divorce, a *hearing* or *status conference* can be scheduled at any time. It is possible you will receive only a few days' notice of a hearing. You will be better prepared for a hearing or a status conference if you have already retained an attorney.

Sample Letter to Spouse

THE LAW FIRM
OF
JOHN F. SCHAEFER
A PROFESSIONAL LIMITED LIABILITY COMPANY
880 NORTH OLD WOODWARD AVENUE, SUITE 820
BIRMINGHAM, MICHIGAN 48009

TELEPHONE (248) 642-6655
TELEFACSIMILE (248) 642-7878
WEBSITE www.lfjfs.com

JOHN F. SCHAEFER ¹
MARK A. BANK ¹·²
B. ANDREW RIFKIN ¹·³
COLLEEN E. JOHNSON
AMANDA D. SZUKALA
ROBERT C. REILAND

WAYNE COUNTY OFFICE
130 KERCHEVAL AVENUE
GROSSE POINTE FARMS, MI 48236
TELEPHONE (313) 881-1300

¹ FELLOW, AMERICAN ACADEMY OF
MATRIMONIAL LAWYERS
² ALSO MEMBER OF MARYLAND, VIRGINIA
AND THE DISTRICT OF COLUMBIA BARS
³ ALSO MEMBER OF COLORADO BAR

[Name]
[Address]
[City, State Zip]

Dear _____:

    I am sorry that our introduction has to take this form; however, I have been retained to represent your husband/wife, _____, in connection with the dissolution of your marriage. I understand it has been troubled for some time. It is _____ desire, and I certainly share it, that this matter be handled with as much privacy and congeniality as possible under the circumstances.

    Obviously, of paramount importance is your child(ren), _____, and his/her/their overall well-being. We know you have an interest in a smooth transition for _____ and we too have this as our primary concern.

    We have elected to write this letter rather than following the common course of filing a complaint for divorce in the _____ Circuit Court thereby bringing about possible public scrutiny. For this less formal process to be effective, we need mutual assurances that the financial *status quo* will be maintained; that is, each of you will conduct your financial affairs as you have in the past. Implicit in that suggestion is that neither of you will change the character of your assets or do anything that might possibly impair the rights of the other party. _____ is prepared to commit to this, and we hope you will similarly concur.

    If the foregoing makes sense to you, I shall appreciate being contacted by your counsel so that we may exchange relevant financial information, conduct any necessary valuations, and proceed to attempt to reach a prompt and acceptable resolution of the matter.

    Thank you for your anticipated cooperation.

Very truly yours,

After your acknowledgment of service has been filed with the court or you have been served by the sheriff or process server, a written answer responding to your spouse's divorce complaint must be filed with the court within twenty-one days if you were served personally or twenty-eight days if you were served by mail or outside the state of Michigan.

1.23   What is an *ex parte court order*?

An *ex parte court order* is obtained by one party going to the judge to ask for something without giving prior notice or an opportunity to be heard by the other side.

With the exception of restraining orders or orders to maintain the *status quo* of the parties, judges are reluctant to sign *ex parte* orders. Ordinarily, the court will require the other side to have notice of any requests for court orders, and a hearing before the judge will be held.

An *affidavit,* which is a written statement sworn under oath, is usually required before a judge will sign an *ex parte* order. *Ex parte* orders are generally limited to emergency situations, such as requests for temporary restraining orders and protection orders.

When an *ex parte* order is granted, the party who did not request the order will have an opportunity to have a subsequent hearing before the judge to determine whether the order should remain in effect.

1.24   What is a *motion*?

A *motion* is a request that the judge enter a court order of some type. For example, your attorney may file a written motion with the court asking for an order related to temporary custody, child support, parenting time, or financial matters, such as payment of bills.

Some motions are made to handle certain procedural aspects of your case, such as a motion for a continuance asking that a court date be changed, or a motion for extension of time asking that the court extend a deadline. In some cases a motion may be made orally rather than in writing, for example when an issue arises during the course of a court hearing or trial.

1.25 Once my complaint for divorce is filed, how soon can a *temporary hearing* be held to decide what happens with our child and our finances while the divorce is pending?

In most cases a *temporary hearing* can be held within thirty days of your divorce being filed with the court, assuming your spouse can be located to be given notice.

1.26 How much notice will I get if my spouse seeks a temporary order?

If your spouse seeks an *ex parte* order, you will not be given notice until the judge has signed the order. All other temporary orders will be requested by motion and set for a hearing in front of the judge. Michigan law requires that you receive at least seven days' notice if served personally, or ten days' notice if served via certified mail, of the filing of a motion and any court hearings.

1.27 During my divorce, what am I responsible for doing?

Your attorney will explain what actions you should take to further the divorce process and to help you reach the best possible outcome.

You will be asked to:

- Keep in regular contact with your attorney.
- Update your attorney regarding any changes in your contact information, such as address, phone numbers, and e-mail address.
- Provide your attorney with all requested documents.
- Provide requested information in a timely manner.
- Complete forms and questionnaires.
- Appear in court on time.
- Be direct about asking any questions you might have.
- Tell your attorney your thoughts on settlement or what you would like the judge to order in your case.
- Remain respectful toward your spouse throughout the process.
- Keep your children out of the litigation.

13

- Comply with any temporary court orders, such as restraining or support orders.
- Advise your attorney of any significant developments in your case.

By doing your part in the divorce process, you enable your attorney to partner with you for a better outcome while also lowering your attorney fees.

1.28 I'm worried that I won't remember to ask my lawyer about all of the issues in my case. How can I be sure I don't miss anything?

Write down all of the topics you want to discuss with your attorney, including what your goals are for the outcome of the divorce. Use the *Divorce Issues Checklist* below as a guide. The sooner you get a clear understanding of your goals, the easier it will be for your attorney to support you to get what you want. Realize that your attorney will think of some issues you may not have thought of. Your lawyer's experience will be helpful in making sure nothing important is forgotten.

Divorce Issues Checklist

Issue	Notes
Dissolution of marriage—divorce	
Custody of minor children	
Removal of children from jurisdiction	
Parenting plan	
Child support	
Deviation from child-support guidelines	
Abatement of child support	
Travel expenses to facilitate parenting time for out-of-town/out-of-state parents	
Life insurance to fund unpaid child support	
Automatic withholding for support	
Child-support arrearage from temporary order	
Child-care expenses	

Divorce Issues Checklist (Continued)

Issue	Notes
Child-care credit	
Health insurance on minor children	
Uninsured medical expenses for minor children	
Qualified medical support order	
Private school tuition for children	
College expenses for children	
College savings accounts for benefit of children	
Health insurance on the parties	
Real property: marital residence	
Real property: rentals, cabins, commercial property	
Time-shares	
Retirement accounts	
Federal or military pensions	
Business interests	
Bank accounts	
Investments	
Stock options	
Stock purchase plans	
Life insurance policies	
Frequent flyer miles	
Credit card points	
Season tickets for events	
Premarital or nonmarital assets	
Premarital or nonmarital debts	
Pets	

Divorce Issues Checklist (Continued)

Issue	Notes
Personal property division: including motor vehicles, recreation vehicles, campers, airplanes, collections, furniture, electronics, tools, household goods	
Exchange date for personal property	
Division of marital debt	
Property settlement	
Alimony	
Life insurance to fund unpaid alimony	
Arrearage of alimony from temporary order	
Tax exemptions for minor children	
IRS form 8332	
Filing status for tax returns for last/current year	
Former name restoration	
Attorney fees	

1.29 My spouse has all of our financial information. How will I be able to prepare for negotiations and trial if I don't know the facts or have the documents?

Once your divorce has been filed with court and temporary matters have been addressed, your attorney will proceed with a process known as *discovery.*

Through discovery, your attorney can ask your spouse to provide documents and information needed to prepare your case. Your attorney can also subpoena information directly from an institution to obtain the requested documentation.

1.30 My spouse and I both want our divorce to be amicable. How can we keep it that way?

You and your spouse are to be commended for your willingness to cooperate while focusing on moving through the divorce process. This will not only make your lives easier and save you money on attorney fees, but it is also more likely to result in an outcome with which you are both satisfied. Find a lawyer who understands your goal to reach settlement and encourage your spouse to do the same. Cooperate with the prompt exchange of necessary information. Then ask your attorney about the options of mediation and negotiation for reaching an agreement. Even if you are not able to settle all of the issues in your divorce, these actions can increase the likelihood of agreement on many of the terms of your divorce decree.

1.31   Can I choose my judge?
You may not choose your own judge or judge "shop." Judge shopping occurs when a person involved in a legal case attempts to influence the court's assignment of a case so that it will be directed to or away from a particular judge. However, talk to your attorney about the reasons you want a different judge. If you believe that your judge has a conflict of interest, such as being a close friend of your spouse, you may have a basis for asking the judge to be "recused" in order to allow another judge to hear the case.

1.32   How long will it take to get my divorce?
The more you and your spouse are in agreement, the faster your divorce will conclude. At a minimum, there will be a sixty-day wait from the date of filing of the divorce complaint.
Assuming all issues, such as custody, support, property, and debts, are completely settled between you and your spouse, if you so choose, a final hearing can be held after the sixty-day waiting period. Otherwise, your decree can be submitted to the judge for his or her approval after the sixty-day waiting period. However, your divorce will still not be "final" for all purposes until the judge signs the judgment of divorce.

1.33   What is the significance of my divorce being final?
The finality of your divorce by a judge's signature on the *judgment of divorce* is important for many reasons. It can affect your right to remarry, your eligibility for health insurance from your former spouse, and your filing status for income taxes.

1.34   When does my divorce become final?
Your divorce becomes final on the day the judge signs your judgment of divorce.

1.35   Can I start using my former name right away, and how do I get my name legally restored?
You may begin using your former name at any time, provided you are not doing so for any unlawful purpose, such as to avoid your creditors. Many agencies and institutions, however, will not alter their records without a court order changing your name.

If you want your former name restored, let your attorney know so that this provision can be included in your divorce judgment. If you want to change your legal name after the divorce and have not provided for it in your judgment, it will be necessary for you to undergo a separate legal action for a name change.

2

Coping with Stress
during the Divorce Process

It may have been a few years ago. Or it may have been many years ago. Perhaps it was only months. But, when you said "I do," you meant it. Like most people getting married, you planned to be a happily married couple for life.

But things happen. Life brings change. People change. Whatever the circumstance, you now find yourself considering divorce. The emotions of divorce run from one extreme to another as you journey through the process. You may feel relief and ready to move on with your life. On the other hand, you may feel emotions that are quite painful. Anger. Fear. Sorrow. A deep sense of loss or failure. Remember, it is important to find support for coping with all these strong emotions.

Because going through a divorce can be an emotional time, having a clear understanding of the divorce process and what to expect will help you make better decisions. And, when it comes to decision making, search inside yourself to clarify your intentions and goals for the future. Let these intentions be your guide.

2.1 My spouse left home weeks ago. I don't want a divorce because I feel our marriage can be saved. Should I still see an attorney?

It's a good idea to see an attorney. Whether you want a divorce or not, there may be important actions for you to take now to protect your assets, credit, home, children, and future right to support.

If your spouse files for divorce, a temporary hearing could be heard in just a matter of days. It is best to be prepared with the support of an attorney, even if you decide not to file for a divorce at this time.

2.2   The thought of going to a lawyer's office to talk about divorce is more than I can bear. I canceled the first appointment I made because I just couldn't do it. What should I do?

Many people going through a divorce are dealing with lawyers for the first time and feel anxious about the experience. Ask a trusted friend or family member to go with you. He or she can support you by writing down your questions in advance, by taking notes for you during the meeting, and by helping you to remember what the lawyer said after the meeting is concluded. It is very likely that you will feel greatly relieved just to be better informed.

2.3   There is some information about my marriage that I think my attorney needs, but I'm too embarrassed to discuss it. Must I tell the attorney?

Your attorney has an ethical duty to maintain confidentiality. Past events in your marriage are matters that your lawyer is obligated to keep private. Attorneys who practice divorce law are accustomed to hearing a lot of intimate information about families. Although it is deeply personal to you, it is unlikely that anything you tell your lawyer will be a shock.

It may feel uncomfortable for a short moment, but it is important that your attorney have complete information so that your interests can be fully protected. If speaking directly about these facts still seems too hard, consider putting them in a letter.

2.4   I'm unsure about how to tell our children about the divorce, and I'm worried I'll say the wrong thing. What's the best way?

How you talk to your children about the divorce will depend upon their ages and development. Changes in your children's everyday lives, such as a change of residence or one parent leaving the home, are far more important to them. Information about legal proceedings and meetings with lawyers are best kept among adults.

Simpler answers are best for young children. Avoid giving them more information than they need. Use the adults in your life as a source of support to meet your own emotional needs.

After the initial discussion with your children, keep the door open to further talks by creating opportunities for them to talk about the divorce. Use these times to acknowledge their feelings and offer support. Always assure them that the divorce is not their fault and that they are still loved by both you and your spouse, regardless of the divorce.

2.5   My youngest child seems very depressed about the divorce, the middle one is angry, and my teenager is skipping school. How can I cope?

A child's reaction to divorce can vary depending upon his or her age and other factors. Some may cry and beg for a reconciliation, and others may behave inappropriately. Reducing conflict with your spouse, being a consistent and nurturing parent, and making sure both of you remain involved with your children are all actions that can support your children regardless of how they are reacting to the divorce.

Support groups for children whose parents are divorcing are available at many schools and religious communities. A school counselor can also provide support. If more help is needed, confer with a therapist experienced in working with children.

2.6   I am so frustrated by my spouse's "Disneyland parent" behavior. Is there anything I can do to stop this?

Feelings of guilt, competition, or remorse sometimes lead a parent to be tempted to spend parenting time in trips to the toy store and special activities. Other times these feelings can result in an absence of discipline in an effort to become the favored parent or to make the time "special."

Shift your focus from the other parent's behavior to your own, and do your best to be an outstanding parent during this time. This includes keeping a routine for your child for family meals, bedtimes, chores, and homework. Encourage family activities, as well as individual time with each child, when it's possible.

During the time when a child's life is changing, providing a consistent and stable routine in your home can ease his or her anxiety and provide comfort.

2.7   Between requests for information from my spouse's lawyer and my own lawyer, I am totally overwhelmed. How do I manage gathering all of this detailed information by the deadlines imposed?

First, simply get started. Often the thought about a task is worse than the job itself.

Second, break it down into smaller tasks. Perhaps one evening you gather your tax returns and on the weekend you work on your monthly living expenses.

Third, let in support. Ask that friend of yours who just loves numbers to come over for an evening with her calculator to help you get organized.

Fourth, communicate with your attorney. Your attorney or paralegal may be able to make your job easier by giving you suggestions or help. It may be that essential information can be provided now and the details submitted later. Any information you are missing may be obtained through discovery questions to your spouse, by subpoena, or simply by making a few phone calls to your financial advisor, banker, or other professional advisors.

2.8   I am so depressed about my divorce that I'm having difficulty getting out of bed in the morning to care for my children. What should I do?

See your health care provider. Feelings of depression are common during a divorce. You also want to make sure that you identify any physical health concerns.

Although feelings of sadness are common during a divorce, more serious depression means it's time to seek professional support.

Your health and your ability to care for your children are both essential. Follow through on recommendations by your health care professionals for therapy, medication, or other measures to improve your wellness.

2.9   Will taking prescribed medication to help treat my insomnia and depression hurt my case?

Not necessarily. Talk to your health care professional and follow their recommendations. Taking care of your health is of the utmost importance during this difficult time and will serve your best interests as well as the best interests of your children. Inform your attorney of any medications that you are taking or treatment that you are seeking.

2.10   I know I need help to cope with the stress of the divorce, but I can't afford counseling. What can I do?

You are wise to recognize that divorce is a time for letting in support. You can explore a number of options, including:

- Meeting with a member of the clergy or lay chaplain
- Joining a divorce support group
- Turning to friends and family members
- Going to a therapist or divorce coach

Depending upon your health care insurance provider, counseling may be covered by your health care insurance. If budget is a concern, contact a social agency that offers counseling services on a sliding-fee scale.

If none of these options are available, look again at your budget. You may see that counseling is important enough that you decide to find a way to increase your income or lower your expenses to support this investment in your well-being.

2.11   I'm the one who filed for divorce, but I still have loving feelings toward my spouse and feel sad about divorcing. Does this mean I should dismiss my divorce?

Strong feelings of caring about your spouse often persist after a divorce is filed. Whether to proceed with a divorce is a deeply personal decision. Although feelings can inform us of our thoughts, sometimes they can also cause us to not look at everything there is to see in our situation.

Have you and your spouse participated in marriage counseling? Has your spouse refused to seek treatment for an addiction? Are you worried about the safety of you or your children if you remain in the marriage? Can you envision yourself as financially secure if you remain in this marriage? Is your spouse involved in another relationship? The answers to these questions can help you get clear about whether to consider reconciliation. Talk to your therapist, coach, or spiritual advisor to help determine the right path for you.

2.12   Will my lawyer charge me for the time I spend talking about my feelings about my spouse and my divorce?

If you are paying your attorney by the hour, expect to be charged for the time your attorney spends talking with you. If your attorney is being paid a flat-fee rate for handling your divorce, the time spent talking with you will be included in the fee. However, the cost should not discourage you from sharing your feelings with your attorney, as it is not only a helpful coping mechanism for you, but it allows your attorney to gather more information that may be helpful to your case.

2. 13 My lawyer doesn't seem to realize how difficult my divorce is for me. How can I get him to understand?

Everyone wants support and compassion from the professionals who help during a divorce. Speak frankly with your attorney about your concerns. It may be that your lawyer does not see your concerns as being relevant to the job of getting your desired outcome in the divorce. Your willingness to improve the communication will help your lawyer understand how best to support you in the process and will help you understand which matters are best left for discussion with your therapist or a supportive friend.

2.14   I've been told not to speak ill of my spouse in front of my child, but I know my spouse is doing this all the time. Why can't I just speak the truth?

It can be devastating for your child to hear you badmouthing his or her other parent. What your child needs is permission to love both of you, regardless of any bad parental behavior. The best way to support your child during this time is to encourage a positive relationship with the other parent.

2.15 Nobody in our family has ever been divorced and I feel really ashamed. Will my children feel the same way?

Making a change in how you see your family identity is huge for you. The best way to help your children is to establish a sense of pride in their new family and to look forward to the future with a real sense of possibility.

Your children will have an opportunity to witness you overcoming obstacles, demonstrating independence, and moving forward in your life notwithstanding challenges. You can be a great teacher to them during this time by demonstrating pride in your family and in yourself.

2.16 I am terrified of having my deposition taken. My spouse's lawyer is very aggressive, and I'm afraid I'm going to say something that will hurt my case.

A *deposition* is an opportunity for your spouse's attorney to gather information and to assess the type of witness you will be if the case proceeds to trial. Feeling anxious about your deposition is normal. However, regardless of the personality of the lawyers, most depositions in divorces are quite uneventful.

Remember that your attorney will be seated by your side at all times to support you. Ask to meet with your lawyer in advance to prepare for the deposition. If you are worried about certain questions that might be asked, talk to your attorney about them. Think of it as an opportunity, and enlist your lawyer's support in being well prepared.

2.17 I am still so angry at my spouse, how can I be expected to sit in the same room during a settlement conference?

If you are still really angry at your spouse, it may be beneficial to postpone the conference if possible. You might also consider seeking some counseling to support you with coping with your feelings of anger.

Prior to the mediation process, ask the mediator to keep you separated from your spouse and his or her attorney as much as possible. Most mediators are willing to grant this request, and many mediators actually prefer keeping the parties separated. Another option might be "shuttle" negotiations. With this method, you and your attorney remain in one room while your spouse and his or her attorney are in another. Settlement offers are then relayed between the attorneys throughout the negotiation process by the mediator. By shifting your focus from your angry feelings to your goal of a settlement, it may be easier to proceed through the process.

2.18   I'm afraid I can't make it through court without having an emotional breakdown. How do I prepare?

A divorce trial can be a highly emotional time, calling for lots of support. Some of these ideas may help you through the process:

- Meet with your lawyer or the firm's support staff in advance of your court date to prepare you for court.
- Ask your lawyer whether there are any documents you should review in preparation for court, such as your deposition.
- Visit the courtroom in advance to get comfortable with the surroundings.
- Ask your lawyer about having a support person with you on your court date.
- Ask yourself what is the worst thing that could happen and consider what options you would have if it did.
- Avoid alcohol, eat healthfully, exercise, and get plenty of rest during the period of time leading up to the court date. Each of these will help you to prepare for the emotions of the day.
- Plan what you intend to wear in advance. Small preparations will lower your stress.
- Visualize the experience going well. Picture yourself sitting in the witness chair, giving clear, confident, and truthful answers to easy questions.
- Arrive early in the courthouse and make sure you have a plan for parking your car if you are not familiar with the area.
- Take slow, deep breaths. Breathing deeply will steady your voice, calm your nerves, and improve your focus.

Coping with Stress during the Divorce Process

Your attorney will be prepared to support you throughout the proceedings. By taking the aforementioned steps, you can increase the ease of your experience.

2.19 I am really confused. One day I think the divorce is a mistake; the next day I know I can't go back, and a few minutes later I can hardly wait to be single again. Some days I just don't believe I'm getting divorced. What's happening?

Denial, transition, and acceptance are common passages for a person going through a divorce. One moment you might feel excited about your future and a few hours later you think your life is ruined.

What can be helpful to remember is that you may not pass from one stage to the next in a direct line. Feelings of anger or sadness may well up in you long after you thought you had moved on. Similarly, your mood might feel bright one day as you think about your future plans, even though you still miss your spouse.

Taking good care of yourself is essential during this period of your life. What you are going through requires a tremendous amount of energy. Allow yourself to experience your emotions, but also continue moving forward with your life. These steps will help your life get easier day by day.

3

Choosing and Working
with Your Attorney

If there is one thing you can be sure of in your divorce,
it's that you will be given plenty of advice. Well-
intentioned neighbors, cousins, and complete strangers will be
happy to tell you war stories about their ex or about their sister
who got divorced in Canada. Many will insist they know what
you should do, even though they know nothing about the facts
of your case or the law in Michigan.

But there is one person whose advice will matter to you:
your attorney. Your lawyer should be your trusted and supportive advocate at all times throughout your divorce. The
counsel of your attorney can affect your life for years to come.
You will never regret taking the time and energy to choose the
right one for you.

See your relationship with your attorney as a partnership
for pursuing what is most important to you. With clear and
open attorney–client communication, you'll have the best outcome possible and your entire divorce will be less stressful.

By working closely with the right lawyer, you can trust
the professional advice you receive and simply thank your
cousin Millie for sharing.

3.1   Where do I begin looking for an attorney for my di-
vorce?

There are many ways to find a divorce lawyer. Ask people you trust—friends and family members who have gone
through a divorce, if they thought they had a good lawyer (or
if their former spouse did!). If you know professionals who

work with attorneys, ask for a referral to an attorney who is experienced in family law.

Consult your local bar association to find out whether they have a referral service. Be sure to specify that you are looking for an attorney who handles divorces.

Check with the local law schools. A faculty member may be able to recommend a lawyer in your area.

Go online. Many attorneys have websites that provide information on their practice areas, professional associations, experience, and philosophy. Lawyers who are listed in *The Best Lawyers in America*, or are members of the American Academy of Matrimonial Lawyers are a good source.

3.2   How do I choose the right attorney?

Choosing the right attorney for your divorce is an important decision. Your attorney should be a trusted professional with whom you feel comfortable sharing information openly. He or she should be a person you can trust and a zealous advocate for your interests.

You will rely upon your attorney to help you make many decisions throughout the course of your divorce. You will also entrust your legal counsel to make a range of strategic and procedural decisions on your behalf.

Consultation for a divorce might be your first meeting with a lawyer. Know that attorneys want to be supportive and to fully inform you. Feel free to seek all of the information you need to help you feel secure in knowing you have made the right choice.

Find an attorney who practices primarily in the family law area. Although many attorneys handle divorces, it is likely you will have more effective representation at a lower cost from an attorney who already knows the fundamentals of divorce law in Michigan.

Determine the level of experience you want in your attorney. For example, if you have had a short marriage, have no children, and few assets, an attorney with lesser experience might be a good value for your legal needs. However, if you are anticipating a custody dispute or have complex or substantial assets, a more experienced attorney may better meet your needs.

Consider the qualities in an attorney that are important to you. Even the most experienced and skilled attorney is not right for every person. Ask yourself what you are really looking for in an attorney so you can make your choice with these standards in mind.

It is important that you be confident in the attorney you hire. If you're unsure about whether the lawyer is really listening to you or understanding your concerns, keep looking until you find one who will. Your divorce is an important matter. It's critical that you have a professional you can trust.

3.3　Should I hire a "bulldog"—a very aggressive attorney?

Again, consider the qualities in an attorney that are important to you. A "bulldog" may promise to be overly aggressive and take your spouse for everything he or she is worth. However, it may be important to you to create a mutually respectful relationship with your spouse during and after the divorce, especially if there are minor children involved.

Additionally, expect the cost of your divorce to exponentially increase if your attorney is unwilling to negotiate and drags your spouse into court at every opportunity. Look for a lawyer who can represent you with zealous advocacy, while at the same time maintaining a high level of courtesy, professionalism, and integrity.

3.4　Should I interview more than one attorney?

Be willing to interview more than one attorney. Every lawyer has different strengths, and it is important that you find the one who is right for you. Sometimes it is only by meeting with more than one attorney that you see clearly who will best be able to help you reach your goals in the way you want.

Changing lawyers in the middle of litigation can be stressful and costly. It is wise to invest energy at the outset in making the right choice.

3.5　My spouse says that because we're still friends we should use the same attorney for the divorce. Is this a good idea?

Even the most amicable of divorcing couples usually have differing interests. For this reason, it is never recommended that an attorney represent both parties to a divorce. In most cases, an attorney is ethically prohibited from representing two people with conflicting interests who are in dispute. Sometimes couples have reached agreements without understanding all of their rights under the law. A party often will benefit from receiving further legal advice on matters such as tax considerations, retirement, and health insurance issues.

It is not uncommon for one party to retain an attorney and for the other party not to do so. In such cases, the party with the attorney files the complaint, and agreements reached between the parties are typically sent to the spouse for approval prior to any court hearing. If your spouse has filed for divorce and said that you do not need an attorney, you should nevertheless meet with a lawyer for advice on how proceeding without a lawyer could affect your legal rights.

3.6   What information should I take with me to the first meeting with my attorney?

Attorneys differ on the amount of information they like to see at an initial consultation. If a court proceeding, either a divorce or a protection order, has already been initiated by either you or your spouse, it is important to take copies of any court documents.

If you have a prenuptial or postnuptial agreement with your spouse, that is another important document for you to bring at the outset of your case.

If you intend to ask for support, either for yourself or for your children, documents evidencing income of both you and your spouse will also be useful. These might include:

- Recent pay stubs
- Individual and business tax returns, W-2s, and 1099s
- Bank statements showing deposits
- A statement of your monthly budget

If your situation is urgent or you do not have access to these documents, don't let it stop you from scheduling your appointment with an attorney. Prompt legal advice about your rights is often more important than having detailed financial information in the beginning. Your attorney can explain to you the options for obtaining these financial records if they are not readily available to you.

3.7 What unfamiliar words might an attorney use at the first meeting?

Law has a language all its own, and attorneys sometimes lapse into "legalese," forgetting that nonlawyers may not recognize words used daily in the practice of law. Some words and phrases you might hear include:

- *Dissolution of marriage*—The divorce
- *Plaintiff*—Person who files the divorce complaint
- *Defendant*—Person who did not file the divorce complaint
- *Jurisdiction*—Authority of a court to make rulings affecting a party
- *Service*—Process of notifying a party about a legal filing
- *Discovery*—Process during which each side provides information to the other
- *Judgment* (or formerly, *decree*)—The final order entered in a divorce

Never hesitate to ask your attorney the meaning of a term. Your complete understanding of your lawyer's advice is essential for you to partner with your advocate as effectively as possible. Additional terms are listed in the Glossary.

3.8 What can I expect at an initial consultation with an attorney?

The nature of the advice you get from an attorney in an initial consultation will depend upon whether you are still deciding whether you want a divorce, whether you are planning for a possible divorce in the future, or whether you are ready to file for divorce right away.

During the meeting, you will have an opportunity to provide the following information to the attorney:

- A brief history of the marriage
- Background information regarding yourself, your spouse, and your children
- Your immediate situation
- Your intentions and goals regarding your relationship with your spouse

- What information you are seeking from the attorney during the consultation

You can expect the attorney to identify the following information to you:

- The procedure for divorce in Michigan
- The issues important in your case
- A preliminary assessment of your rights and responsibilities under the law
- Background information regarding the firm
- Information about fees and filings

Although some questions may be impossible for the attorney to answer at the initial consultation because additional information or research is needed, the initial consultation is an opportunity for you to ask all of the questions you have at the time of the meeting.

3.9 Will the communication with my attorney be confidential?

Yes. Your lawyer has an ethical duty to maintain your confidentiality. This duty of confidentiality also extends to the legal staff working with your attorney. The privileged information that you share with your attorney will remain private and confidential, unless such privilege is waived by voluntarily disclosing it to third parties.

3.10 Is there any way that I could accidentally waive the attorney–client privilege as it relates to the duty of confidentiality?

Yes. To ensure that communications between you and your attorney remain confidential, and to protect against the voluntary or involuntary waiver of such privilege, consider the following tips:

- Refrain from disclosing the content of the communications with your attorney or discussing in substantive detail the communications with your attorney with third parties. Such third parties can include friends and family members.
- Social media provides the potential for waiving the attorney–client privilege by publicly disclosing confi-

33

dential information. Do not post information or send messages relating to your case on Facebook, Twitter, or other social media websites.

• Do not post information relating to your case or communications with your attorney on a personal blog, video blog, online chat rooms, or online message boards.

• Do not use your work-related e-mail to communicate with your attorney or to discuss your case.

• Depending upon your employer's policy relating to electronic communication, the attorney–client privilege may be waived by communicating with your attorney or by discussing your case through your personal e-mail account (Gmail, Yahoo, etc.) through a company computer. To ensure your communications remain confidential, it is best to communicate only through e-mail from your private e-mail address from your home computer that's not shared with other family members.

3.11 Can I take a friend or family member to my initial consultation?

Yes. Having someone present during your initial consultation can be a source of great support. You might ask him or her to take notes on your behalf so that you can focus on listening and asking questions. Remember that this is your consultation, however, and it is important that the attorney hears the facts of your case directly from you. It is very important, however, to ask your attorney how having a third party present at your consultation could impact the attorney–client privilege. There may be times when the third party should be excused from the meeting.

3.12 What exactly will my attorney do to help me get a divorce?

Your attorney will play a critical role in helping you get your divorce. You will be actively involved in some of the work, while other actions will occur behind the scenes at the law office, the law library, or the courthouse.

Your attorney may perform any of the following tasks on your behalf:

- Assess the case to determine which court has jurisdiction to hear your divorce.
- Develop a strategy for advising you about all aspects of your divorce, including the treatment of assets and matters concerning children.
- Prepare legal documents for filing with the court.
- Conduct discovery to obtain information from the other party, which could include depositions, requests for production of documents, and written interrogatories.
- Appear with you at all court appearances, depositions, and conferences.
- Schedule all deadlines and court appearances.
- Support you in responding to information requests from your spouse.
- Inform you of actions you are required to take.
- Perform financial analyses of your case.
- Conduct legal research.
- Prepare you for court appearances and depositions.
- Prepare your case for hearings and trial, including preparing exhibits and interviewing witnesses.
- Advise you regarding your rights under the law.
- Counsel you regarding the risks and benefits of negotiated settlement as compared to proceeding to trial.

As your advocate, your attorney is entrusted to take all of the steps necessary to represent your interests in the divorce.

3.13 What professionals should I expect to work with during my divorce?

Depending upon the issues identified by your attorney, you can expect to work with various types of professionals, such as appraisers, financial professionals, real estate agents, and mental health experts.

Additionally, in some cases where custody or parenting time issues are seriously disputed, the court may appoint a *guardian ad litem (GAL)*. This person, usually a lawyer, has the duty to represent the best interests of the child. A guardian *ad litem* has the responsibility to investigate you and your spouse as well as the needs of your child. She or he may then be called as a witness at trial to testify regarding any relevant observations.

Another expert who could be appointed by the court is a psychologist. The role of the psychologist will depend upon the purpose for which she or he is appointed. For example, the psychologist may be appointed to perform a child-custody evaluation, which involves assessing both parents and the child, or this expert may be ordered to evaluate one parent to assess the child's safety while spending time with that parent.

3.14 I've been divorced before and I don't think I need an attorney this time; however, my spouse is hiring one. Is it wise to go it alone?

Having gone through a prior divorce, it's likely that you have learned a great deal about the divorce process as well as your legal rights. However, there are many reasons why you should be extremely cautious about proceeding without legal representation.

It is important to remember that every divorce is different. The length of the marriage, whether there are children, the relative financial situation of you and your spouse, as well as your age and health can all affect the financial outcome in your divorce.

The law may have changed since your last divorce. Some aspects of divorce law are likely to change each year. New laws get passed and new decisions get handed down by the Michigan Supreme Court and the Michigan Court of Appeals that affect the rights and responsibilities of people who divorce.

In some cases, the involvement of your lawyer could be minimal. This might be the case if your marriage was short, your financial situation very similar to that of your spouse, there are no children, and the two of you remain amicable. At a minimum, have an initial consultation with an attorney to discuss your rights and have an attorney review any final agreement.

3.15   Can I bring my children to meetings with my attorney?

It's best to make other arrangements for your children when you meet with your attorney. Your attorney will be giving you a great deal of important information during your conferences, and it will benefit you to give your full attention.

It's also recommended that you take every measure to keep information about the legal aspects of your divorce away from your children. Knowledge that you are seeing an attorney can add to your child's anxiety about the process. It can also make your child a target for questioning by the other parent about your contacts with your attorney.

Most law offices are not designed to accommodate young children and are ordinarily not "child-proof." For both your child's well-being and your own peace of mind, explore options for someone to care for your child when you have meetings with your attorney.

3.16   What is the role of the *paralegal* or *legal assistant* in my attorney's office?

A *paralegal,* or *legal assistant,* is a trained legal professional whose duties include providing support for you and your lawyer. Working with a paralegal can make your divorce easier because he or she is likely to be very available to help you. It can also lower your legal costs because the hourly rate for paralegal services is less than the rate for attorneys.

A paralegal is prohibited from giving legal advice. It is important that you respect the limits of the role of the paralegal if he or she is unable to answer your question because it calls for giving a legal opinion. However, a paralegal can answer many questions and provide a great deal of information to you throughout your divorce.

Paralegals can help you by receiving information from you, reviewing documents with you, providing you with updates on your case, and answering questions about the divorce process that do not call for legal advice.

3.17 My attorney is not returning my phone calls. What can I do?

You have a right to expect your phone calls to be returned by your lawyer. Here are some options to consider:

- Ask to speak to the paralegal or another attorney in the office.

- Send an e-mail or fax telling your lawyer that you have been trying to reach him or her by phone and explaining the reason it is important that you receive a call.

- Ask the receptionist to schedule a phone conference for you to speak with your attorney at a specific date and time.

- Schedule a meeting with your attorney to discuss both the issue needing attention as well as your concerns about the communication.

Your attorney wants to provide good service to you. If your calls are not being returned, take action to get the communication with your lawyer back on track.

3.18 How do I know when it's time to change lawyers?

Changing lawyers is costly. You will incur legal fees for your new attorney to review information that is already familiar to your current attorney. You will spend time giving much of the same information to your new lawyer that you gave to the one you have discharged. A change in lawyers often results in delays in the divorce.

The following are questions to ask yourself when you're deciding whether to stay with your attorney or seek new counsel:

- Have I spoken directly to my attorney about my concerns?

- When I expressed concerns, did my lawyer take action accordingly?

- Is my lawyer open and receptive to what I have to say?

- Am I blaming my lawyer for bad behavior of my spouse or opposing counsel?

- Have I provided my lawyer the information needed for taking the next action?
- Does my lawyer have control over the complaints I have, or are they ruled by the law or the judge?
- Is my lawyer keeping promises for completing action on my case?
- Do I trust my lawyer?
- What would be the advantages of changing lawyers when compared to the cost?
- Do I believe my lawyer will support me to achieve the outcome I'm seeking in my divorce?

Every effort should be made to resolve concerns with your attorney. If you have made this effort and the situation remains unchanged, it may be time to switch lawyers.

3.19   Are there certain expectations that I should have when working with my legal team?

Yes. Your legal team will be able to provide you with support and guidance during the divorce process. There are certain actions you can expect your legal team to do for you during your divorce, such as:

Meet with you prior to the filing of a court action to advise you on actions you should take first. There may be important steps to take before you initiate the legal process. Your legal team can support you to be well prepared prior to initiating divorce.

Take action to obtain a temporary court order or to enforce existing orders. Temporary court orders are often needed to ensure clarity regarding rights and responsibilities while your divorce is pending. Your legal team can help you obtain a temporary order and ask the court to enforce its orders if there is a violation.

Explain the legal process during each step of your case. Understanding the legal process reduces the stress of your divorce. Your legal team can guide you each step of the way.

Listen to your concerns and answer any questions. Although only the attorneys can give you legal advice, everyone on your team is available to listen, to provide support, and to direct you to the right person who can help.

Support you in developing your parenting plan. Many parents do not know how to decide what type of parenting plan is best for their children. Your legal team can help you look at the needs of your children and offer advice based on their experience in working with families.

Support you in the completion of your discovery responses and preparing for depositions. The discovery process can be overwhelming for anyone. You will be asked to provide detailed information and many documents. Your legal team can make this job easier. Just ask. If your case involves depositions, your legal team will support you to be fully prepared for the experience.

Identify important issues, analyze the evidence, and advise you. Divorce is complex. Often there is a great deal of uncertainty. Your legal team can analyze the unique facts of your case and advise you based upon the law and their expertise.

Communicate with the opposing party's attorney to try to resolve issues without going to court and to keep your case progressing. Although your attorney cannot control the actions of the opposing party or their lawyer, your attorney can always initiate communication as your advocate. Phoning, e-mailing, or writing to opposing counsel are actions your legal team can take to encourage cooperation and to keep your divorce moving forward at the pace you want without the expense of contested litigation.

Think creatively regarding challenges with your case and provide options for your consideration. At the outset, you may see many obstacles to reaching a final resolution. Your legal team can offer creative ideas for resolving challenges and help you to explore your options to achieve the best possible outcome.

Facilitate the settlement process. Although your legal team can never make the other party settle, your attorney can take action to promote settlement. They can prepare settlement proposals, invite settlement conferences, and negotiate zealously on your behalf.

3.20 Are there certain things my legal team will not be able to do?

Yes. Although there are many ways in which your legal team can support you during your divorce, there are also things your legal team will not be able to accomplish, such as:

Force the other parent to exercise their parenting time. Your legal team cannot force a parent to exercise parenting time. However, be mindful that a chronic neglect of parenting time may be a basis for modifying your parenting plan. Tell your attorney if the other parent is repeatedly failing to exercise their parenting time.

Force the other party to respond to a settlement proposal. Your attorney may send proposals or make requests to opposing counsel; however, there is no duty to respond. After repeated follow-ups without a response, it may be clear no response is coming. At that time, your attorney will decide whether the issues merit court action. Both parties must agree on all terms for a case to be settled without a trial. If one party wants to proceed to trial, even over a single issue, he or she will be able to do so.

Control the tone of communication from opposing counsel or communications from the other party, or the other party's family members. Unfortunately, communication from the opposing attorney may sometimes appear rude, condescending, or demanding. Your legal team cannot stop an attorney from using these tactics.

Absent a pattern of harassment, your legal team cannot stop the other party or third parties from contacting you. If you do not want the contact, talk with your attorney about how to best handle the situation. Of course, appropriate communication regarding your children is always encouraged.

Ask the court to compensate you for every wrong done to you by the other party over the course of your marriage. Although your attorney will empathize that you do have valid complaints, please understand that focusing on the most important issues will yield the best outcome in the end. Raising numerous small issues may distract from your most important goals.

Remedy poor financial decisions made during the marriage. With few exceptions, the court's duty is to divide the marital estate as it currently exists. The judge will not attempt to remedy all past financial wrongs, such as overspending or poor investments by your spouse. If there is significant debt, consult with a debt counselor or bankruptcy lawyer.

Control how the other party parents your children during his or her parenting time. Each parent has strengths and weaknesses. Absent special needs of a child, most judges will not issue orders regarding bedtimes, amount of TV watching or playing video games, discipline methods, clothing, or diet. Of course, any suspected abuse should be reported immediately to the appropriate authorities.

Demand an accounting of how a parent uses court-ordered child support. Absent extraordinary circumstances, the court will not order the other parent to provide an accounting for the use of child support.

Leveraging money for rights regarding your children. Tactics oriented toward asserting custody rights as leverage toward attaining financial goals will be discouraged. Your legal team should negotiate parenting issues based solely on considerations related to your child, then, separately negotiate child support based on financial considerations.

Guarantee payment of child support and alimony. Enforcement of payment of support is possible only when it is court ordered. However, even with a court order, you may experience inconsistent timing of payment due to job loss or a refusal to pay. Talk with your attorney if a pattern of repeated missed payments has developed.

Collect child care and uninsured medical expenses if provisions of the decree are not complied with. If your decree requires you to provide documentation of payment of expenses to the other party and you fail to, you could be prohibited from collecting reimbursement for those expenses. Follow the court's orders regarding providing documentation to the other parent, even if they don't pay as they should. Always keep records of these expenses and payments made by each parent, and keep copies of communications with the other parent regarding payment/reimbursement. It is much easier to keep these records on an ongoing basis than to get copies of old checks, child-care bills, medical bills, and insurance documents at a later time.

4

Attorney Fees and Costs

Any time you make a major investment, you want to know what the cost is going to be and what you are getting for your money. Investing in quality legal representation for your divorce is no different.

The cost of your divorce might be one of your greatest concerns. Because of this, you will want to be an intelligent consumer of legal services. You want quality, but you also want to get the best value for the fees you are paying.

Legal fees for a divorce can be costly and the total expense not always predictable. But there are many actions you can take to control and estimate the cost. Develop a plan early on for how you will finance your divorce. Speak openly with your lawyer about fees from the outset. Learn as much as you can about how you will be charged. Insist on a written fee agreement.

By being informed, aware, and wise, your financial investment in your divorce will be money well spent to protect your future.

4.1 Can I get free legal advice from a lawyer over the phone?

Every law firm has its own policy regarding their lawyers talking to people who are not yet clients of the firm. Most questions about your divorce are too complex for a lawyer to give a meaningful answer during a brief phone call.

Questions about your divorce require a complete look at the facts, circumstances, and background of your marriage. To obtain good legal advice, it's best to schedule an initial consultation with a lawyer who handles divorces.

4.2 Will I be charged for an initial consultation with a lawyer?

It depends. Some lawyers give free consultations, while others charge a fee. When scheduling your appointment, you should be told the amount of the fee. Payment is ordinarily due at the time of the consultation.

4.3 If I decide to hire an attorney, when do I have to pay him or her?

If your attorney charges for an initial consultation, be prepared to make payment at the time of your meeting. At the close of your consultation, the attorney may tell you the amount of the retainer needed by the law firm to handle your divorce. However, you are not expected to pay the retainer at the time of your first meeting. Rather, the retainer is paid after the lawyer has accepted your case, you have decided to hire the lawyer, and you are ready to proceed.

4.4 What exactly is a *retainer,* and how much will mine be?

A *retainer* is a sum paid to your lawyer in advance for services to be performed and costs to be incurred in your divorce. Sometimes it is a minimum fee for the case. It may be an amount paid toward a "flat fee" for your divorce, or an advance credit for services that will be charged by the hour, or a payment in anticipation of results obtained.

If your case is accepted by the law firm, expect the attorney to request a retainer following the initial consultation. The amount of the retainer may vary from hundreds of dollars to many thousands of dollars, depending upon the nature of your case. Contested custody, divorces involving businesses or interstate disputes, for example, are all likely to require higher retainers.

Other factors that can affect the amount of the retainer include the nature and number of the disputed issues.

4.5 Will my attorney accept my divorce case on a *contingency-fee* basis?

No. A *contingency fee* is one that is a specific percentage of your award. In Michigan, lawyers are prohibited from entering into a contingent fee contract in any domestic-relations matter. The amount of alimony or spousal support awarded, or the award of assets as part of the division of the marital estate, however, may be important in discussing results obtained. Sometimes in particularly complex matters, attorneys and clients agree that results are the more important factor, and the client wishes to compensate the attorney, within the client's sole discretion, for extraordinary results.

4.6 How much does it cost to get a divorce?

The cost of your divorce will depend upon many factors. Some attorneys perform divorces for a flat fee, but most charge by the hour, or a combination of hourly charges and results. A *flat fee* is a fixed amount for the legal services being provided. A flat fee is more likely to be used when there are no children of the marriage and the parties have agreed upon the division of their property and debts. Most Michigan attorneys charge by the hour for divorces; however, in extremely complex high-end matters, results are often a factor.

It is important that your discussion of the cost of your divorce begin at your first meeting with your attorney. As mentioned earlier, it is customary for family law attorneys to request a retainer, also known as a *fee advance,* prior to beginning work on your case.

Be sure to ask your attorney what portion, if any, of the retainer is refundable if you do not continue with the case or if you terminate your relationship with the attorney. Sometimes it is nonrefundable.

4.7 What are typical hourly rates for a divorce lawyer?

In Michigan, attorneys who practice in the divorce area charge from $100 per hour to $700 per hour. The rate your attorney charges may depend upon factors such as skills, reputation, experience, exclusive focus on divorce law, and what other attorneys in the area are charging.

If you have a concern about the amount of an attorney's hourly rate, but you would like to hire the firm with which the attorney is associated, consider asking to work with an *associate attorney* in the firm who is likely to charge a lower rate. Associates are attorneys who ordinarily have less experience than the senior partners. However, they often are trained by the senior partners, are very experienced, and are fully capable of handling your case.

4.8   If I can't afford to pay the full amount of the retainer, can I make monthly payments to my attorney?

Every law firm has its own policies regarding payment arrangements for divorce clients. Often these arrangements are tailored to the specific client. Most attorneys will require a substantial retainer to be paid at the outset of your case. Some attorneys may accept monthly payments in lieu of the retainer. Most will require monthly payments in addition to the initial retainer or request additional retainers as your case progresses. Ask frank questions of your attorney to have clarity about your responsibility for payment of legal fees.

4.9   I agreed to pay my attorney a substantial retainer to begin my case. Will I still have to make monthly payments?

Ask your attorney what will be expected of you regarding payments on your account while the divorce is in progress. Clarify whether monthly payments on your account will be expected, whether it is likely that you will be asked to pay additional retainers, and whether the firm charges interest on past-due accounts. Regular payments to your attorney can help you avoid having a tremendously burdensome legal bill at the end of your case. Additionally, you may also be required to keep a minimum credit balance on your account to ensure your case is adequately funded for ongoing work by your legal team.

4.10 My lawyer gave me an estimate of the cost of my divorce and it sounds reasonable. Do I still need a written fee agreement?

Absolutely. Insist upon a written agreement with your attorney. This is essential not only to define the scope of the services for which you have hired your lawyer, but also to ensure that you have clarity about matters such as your attorney's hourly rate, whether you will be billed for certain costs such as copying, and when you can expect to receive statements on your account.

A clear fee agreement reduces the risk of misunderstandings between you and your lawyer. It supports you both in being clear about your promises to each other so that your focus can be on the legal services being provided rather than on disputes about your fees.

4.11 How will I know how the fees and charges are accumulating?

Be sure your written fee agreement with your attorney is completely clear about how you will be informed regarding the status of your account. If your attorney agrees to handle your divorce for a flat fee, your fee agreement should clearly set forth what is included in the fee.

Many attorneys charge by the hour for handling divorces. At the outset of your case, be sure your written fee agreement includes a provision for the attorney to provide you with regular statements of your account. It is reasonable to ask that these be provided monthly.

Review the statement of your account promptly after you receive it. Check to make sure there are no errors, such as duplicate billing entries. If your statement reflects work that you were unaware was performed, call for clarification. Your attorney's office should welcome any questions you have about services it provided.

Your statement might also include filing fees, court reporter fees for transcripts of court testimony or depositions, copy expenses, or interest charged on your account. If several weeks have passed and you have not received a statement on your account, call your attorney's office to request one. Legal fees can mount quickly, and it is important that you stay aware of the status of your legal expenses.

4.12 What other expenses are related to the divorce litigation besides lawyer fees?

Talk to your attorney about costs other than the attorney fees. Ask whether it is likely there will be fees for filing, court reporter expenses, subpoenas, expert witnesses, mediation, or parenting classes. Expert witness fees can be a substantial expense, ranging from hundreds to many thousands of dollars, depending upon the type of expert and the extent to which he or she is involved in your case.

Speak frankly with your attorney about these costs so that together you can make the best decisions about how to use your budget for the litigation.

4.13 Who pays for the experts such as appraisers, accountants, psychologists, and mediators?

Costs for the services of experts, whether appointed by the court or hired by the parties, are ordinarily paid for by the parties.

In the case of the guardian *ad litem* who may be appointed to represent the best interests of your children, the amount of the fee will depend upon how much time this professional spends. The judge often orders this fee to be shared by the parties equally or commensurate with their respective levels of income. However, depending upon the circumstances, one party can be ordered to pay the entire fee. If you can demonstrate *indigency,* that is, a very low income and no ability to pay, the county may be ordered to pay your share of the guardian *ad litem* fee.

Psychologists either charge by the hour or set a flat fee for a certain type of evaluation. Again, the court can order one party to pay this fee or both parties to share the expense. It is not uncommon for a psychologist to request payment in advance and hold the release of an expert report until fees are paid.

Mediators either charge a flat fee per session or an hourly rate fee. Generally, each party will pay one-half of the mediator's fee, which is paid prior to your mediation sessions.

The fees for many experts, including appraisers and accountants, will vary depending upon whether the individuals are called upon to provide only a specific service such as an appraisal, or whether they will need to prepare for giving testimony and appear as a witness at trial.

4.14 What factors will impact how much my divorce will cost?

Although it is difficult to predict how much your legal fees will be, the following are some of the factors that affect the cost:

- Whether there are children
- Whether child custody is agreed upon
- Whether there are novel legal questions
- The complexity of the assets to be divided
- The nature of the issues contested
- The number of issues agreed to by the parties
- The cooperation of the opposing party and opposing counsel
- The frequency of your communication with your legal team
- The ability of the parties to communicate with each other, as well as the client's ability to communicate with her attorney
- The promptness with which information is provided and/or exchanged between both the clients and the attorneys
- Whether there are litigation costs, such as fees for expert witnesses or court reporters
- The hourly rate of the attorney
- The time it will take to conclude your divorce
- Extensive travel needed

Communicating with your lawyer regularly about your legal fees will help you to have a better understanding of the overall cost as your case proceeds.

Divorce in Michigan

4.15 Will my attorney charge for phone calls and e-mails?

Unless your case is being handled on a flat-fee basis, you should expect to be billed for any communication with your attorney. Many of the professional services provided by lawyers are done by phone and by e-mail. This time can be spent giving legal advice, negotiation, or gathering information to protect your interests. These calls and e-mails are all legal services for which you should anticipate being charged by your attorney.

To make the most of your time during attorney phone calls, plan your call in advance. Organize the information you want to relay, your questions, and any concerns to be addressed. This will help you to be clear and focused during the phone call so that your fees are well spent.

4.16 Will I be charged for talking to the staff at my lawyer's office?

It depends. Check the terms of your fee agreement with your lawyer. Whether you are charged fees for talking to nonlawyer members of the law office may depend upon their role in the office. For example, many law firms charge for the services of paralegals and law clerks.

Remember that nonlawyers cannot give legal advice, so it is important to respect their roles. Don't expect the receptionist to give you an opinion regarding whether you will win custody or receive alimony.

Your lawyer's support staff will be able relay your messages and receive information from you. They may also be able to answer many of your questions. Allowing this type of support from within the firm is an important way to control your legal fees, too.

4.17 What is a *litigation budget,* and how do I know if I need one?

If your case is complex and you are anticipating substantial legal fees, ask your attorney to prepare a *litigation budget* for your review. This can help you to understand the nature of the services anticipated, the time that may be spent, and the overall amount it will cost to proceed to trial. The litigation budget will likely be composed of a combination of your attorney and your legal team's hourly rates. It can also be helpful for budgeting and planning for additional retainers. Knowing the anticipated costs of litigation can help you to make meaningful decisions about which issues to litigate and which to consider resolving through settlement negotiations.

4.18   What is a *trial retainer,* and will I have to pay one?

The purpose of the *trial retainer* is to fund the work needed to prepare for trial and for services the day or days of trial. A trial retainer is a sum of money paid on your account with your lawyer when it appears as though your case may not settle and is at risk for proceeding to trial.

Confirm with your attorney that any unearned portion of your trial retainer will be refunded if your case settles. Ask your lawyer whether and when a trial retainer might be required in your case so that you can avoid surprises and plan your budget accordingly.

4.19   How do I know whether I should spend the attorney fees my lawyer says it will require to take my case to trial?

Deciding whether to take a case to trial or to settle is often the most challenging point in the divorce process. This decision should be made with the support of your attorney.

When the issues in dispute are primarily financial, often the decision about settlement is related to the costs of going to trial. Examine how far apart you and your spouse are on financial matters and compare this to the estimated costs of going to trial. By comparing these amounts, you can decide whether a compromise on certain financial issues and certainty about the outcome would be better than paying legal fees and not knowing how your case will resolve.

4.20   Is there any way I can reduce some of the expenses of getting a divorce?

Litigation of any kind can be expensive, and divorces are no exception. The good news is that there are many ways that you can help control the expense, including the following:

Put it in writing. If you need to relay information that is important but not urgent, consider providing it to your attor-

Divorce in Michigan

ney by mail, fax, or e-mail. This creates a prompt and accurate record for your file and takes less time than exchanging phone messages and talking on the phone.

Keep your attorney informed. Just as your attorney should keep you up to date on the status of your case, you need to do the same. Keep your lawyer advised about any major developments in your life such as plans to move, have someone move into your home, change your employment status, or buy or sell property.

During your divorce, if your contact information changes, be sure to notify your attorney. Your attorney may need to reach you with information, and reaching you in a timely manner may help avoid more costly fees later.

Obtain copies of documents. An important part of litigation includes reviewing documents such as tax returns, account statements, report cards, or medical records. Your attorney will ordinarily be able to request or subpoena these items, but many may be readily available to you directly upon request.

Consult your attorney's website. If your lawyer has a website, it may be a great source of useful information. The answers to commonly asked questions about the divorce process can often be found there.

Utilize support professionals. Get to know the support staff at your lawyer's office. Although only attorneys are able to give you legal advice, the receptionist, paralegal, legal secretary, or law clerk may be able to answer your questions regarding the status of your case. Just as your communication with your attorney, all communication with any professionals in a law firm is required to be kept strictly confidential.

Consider working with an associate attorney. Although the senior attorneys or partners in a law firm may have more experience, you may find that working with an associate attorney is a good option. Hourly rates for an associate attorney are typically lower than those charged by a senior partner. Frequently, the associate attorney has trained under a senior partner and developed excellent skills, as well as knowledge of the law. Many associate attorneys are also very experienced.

Discuss with the firm the benefits of working with a senior or an associate attorney in light of the nature of your case,

52

the expertise of the respective attorneys, and the potential cost savings to you.

Leave a detailed message. If your attorney knows the information you are seeking, she or he can often get the answer before returning your call. This not only gets your answer faster, but also reduces costs.

Discuss more than one matter during a call. It is not unusual for clients to have many questions during litigation. If your question is not urgent, consider waiting to call until you have more than one inquiry. Never hesitate to call to ask any legal questions.

Provide timely responses to information requests. Whenever possible, provide information requested by your lawyer in a timely manner. This avoids the cost of follow-up action by your lawyer and the additional expense of extending the time in litigation.

Carefully review your monthly statements. Scrutinize your monthly billing statements closely. If you believe an error has been made, contact your lawyer's office right away to discuss your concerns.

Remain open to settlement. Be alert to recognize that when your disagreement concerns financial matters, the value of money in dispute may be less than the amount it will cost to go to trial. By doing your part, you can use your legal fees wisely and control the costs of your divorce.

4.21 I don't have any money and I need a divorce. What are my options?

If you have a low income and few assets, you may be eligible to obtain a divorce at no cost or minimal cost through one of the following organizations:

- Legal Aid and Defender—Metro Detroit
- Detroit Free Legal Aid Clinic
- Michigan State Bar Association Lawyer Referral/Legal Services

These organizations have a screening process for potential clients, as well as limits on the nature of the cases they take. The demand for their services is also usually greater than the number of attorneys available to handle cases. Consequently, if you are eligible for legal services from one of these programs, you should anticipate being on a waiting list. In short, if you have very little income and few assets, you are likely to experience some delay in obtaining a lawyer. If you believe you might be eligible for participation in one of these programs, inquire early to increase your opportunity to get the legal help you are seeking.

4.22 I don't have much money, but I need to get a divorce as quickly as possible. What should I do?

If you have some money and want to divorce as soon as possible, consider some of these options:

- Borrow the legal fees from friends or family. Often, those close to you are concerned about your future and would be pleased to support you in your goal of having your rights protected. Although this may be uncomfortable to do, remember that most people will appreciate that you trusted them enough to ask for their help. If the retainer is too much money to request from a single individual, consider whether a handful of persons might each be able to contribute a lesser amount to help you reach your goal of hiring a lawyer.

- Charge the legal fees on a low-interest credit card or consider taking out a loan.

- Start saving. If your case is not urgent, consider developing a plan for saving the money you need to proceed with a divorce. Your attorney may be willing to receive and hold monthly payments until you have paid an amount sufficient to pay the initial retainer.

- Talk to your attorney about using money held in a joint account with your spouse.

- Find an attorney who will work with you on a monthly payment basis.

- Ask your attorney about your spouse paying for your legal fees

- Ask your attorney about his or her being paid from the proceeds of the property settlement. If you and your spouse have acquired substantial assets during the marriage, you may be able to find an attorney who will wait to be paid until the assets are divided at the conclusion of the divorce.

Closely examine all sources of funds readily available to you because you may have overlooked money that might be easily accessible to you.

Even if you do not have the financial resources to proceed with your divorce at this time, consult with an attorney to learn your rights and to develop an action plan for steps you can take between now and the time you are able to proceed.

Often there are measures you can take right away to protect yourself until you have the money to proceed with your divorce.

4.23   Is there anything I can do on my own to get support for my children if I don't have money for a lawyer for a divorce?

Yes. If you need support for your children, contact the Michigan Friend of the Court (FOC) in your county for help in obtaining a child-support order. You also may apply for child support online through MiChildSupport, a division of the Department of Human Resources, by visiting their website at https://micase.state.mi.us/ssoapp/login.

4.24   If my mother pays my legal fees, will my lawyer give her private information about my divorce?

If someone else is paying your legal feels, discuss with your lawyer and the payor your expectations that your lawyer will honor the ethical duty of confidentiality. Without your permission, your attorney should not disclose information to others about your case.

However, if you authorize your attorney to speak with your family members, be aware that you will be charged for these communications. Regardless of the opinions of the person who pays your attorney fees, your lawyer's duty is to remain your zealous advocate.

4.25 Can I ask the court to order my spouse to pay my attorney fees?

Yes. If you want to ask the court to order your spouse to pay any portion of your legal fees, be sure to discuss this with your attorney at the first opportunity. Most lawyers will treat the obligation for your legal fees as yours until the other party has made payment.

If your case is likely to require costly experts and your spouse has a much greater ability to pay these expenses than you, talk to your lawyer about the possibility of filing a motion with the court asking your spouse to pay toward these costs while the case is pending.

4.26 What happens if I don't pay my attorney the fees I promised to pay?

The ethical rules for lawyers allow your attorney to withdraw from representation if you do not comply with your fee agreement. Your attorney may also file an attorney's lien against any judgment awarded to you to pay any outstanding attorney's fees or costs to the firm. Consequently, it is important that you keep the promises you have made regarding your account.

If you are having difficulty paying your attorney's fees, talk with your attorney about payment options. Consider borrowing the funds, using your credit card, or asking for help from friends and family.

Above all, do not avoid communication with your attorney if you are having challenges making payment. Keeping in touch with your attorney is essential for you to have an advocate at all stages of your divorce.

5

The Discovery Process

Discovery is one of the least talked about steps in divorce, but it is often among the most important. *Discovery* is the pretrial phase in a lawsuit during which each party can obtain evidence from the opposing party or third parties. The purpose of discovery is to ensure that both you and your spouse have access to the same information. In this way, you can either negotiate a fair agreement or have all of the facts and documents to present to the judge at trial. The discovery process enables you and your spouse to meet on a more level playing field when it comes to settling your case or taking it to trial. You and your spouse both need the same information if you hope to reach agreement on any of the issues in your divorce. Similarly, a judge must know all of the facts to make a fair decision.

The discovery process may seem tedious at times because of the need to obtain and to provide lots of detailed information. Completing it, however, can give tremendous clarity about the issues in your divorce. Trust your lawyer's advice about the importance of having the necessary evidence as you complete the discovery process in order to reach your goals in your divorce.

5.1 What types of discovery might be done by my lawyer or my spouse's lawyer?

Types of discovery include:

- *Interrogatories*—which are written questions that must be answered under oath

57

- *Requests for production of documents*—asking that certain documents be provided by you or your spouse
- *Requests for admissions*—asking that certain facts be admitted or denied
- *Subpoena of documents*—court order requesting documentation or verbal testimony from a person or entity
- *Depositions*—in which questions are asked and answered in the presence of a court reporter but outside the presence of a judge

Factors that can influence the type of discovery conducted in your divorce can include:

- The types of issues in dispute
- How much access you and your spouse have to needed information
- The level of cooperation in sharing information
- The budget available for performing discovery

Talk to your lawyer about the nature and extent of discovery anticipated in your case.

5.2   How long does the discovery process take?

Discovery can take anywhere from a few weeks to a number of months, depending upon factors such as the complexity of the case, the cooperation of you and your spouse, and whether expert witnesses are involved.

The Michigan Court Rules provide that interrogatories, requests for production of documents, and requests for admissions must be responded to within twenty-eight days.

5.3   My lawyer insists that we conduct discovery, but I don't want to spend the time and money on it. Is it really necessary?

The discovery process can be critical to a successful outcome in your case for several reasons:

- It increases the likelihood that any agreements reached are based on accurate information.
- It provides necessary information for deciding whether to settle or proceed to trial.

- It supports the preparation of defenses by providing information regarding your spouse's care.
- It avoids surprises at trial, such as unexpected witness testimony.
- It ensures all potential issues are identified by your attorney.

Discuss with your attorney the intention behind the discovery being conducted in your case to ensure it is consistent with your goals and a meaningful investment of your legal fees.

5.4   I just received from my spouse's attorney interrogatories and requests that I produce documents. My lawyer wants me to respond within two weeks. I'll never make the deadline. What can I do?

Answering your discovery promptly will help move your case forward and help control your legal fees. There are steps you can take to make this task easier.

First, look at all of the questions. Many of them will not apply or your answers will be a simple "yes" or "no."

Ask a friend to help you. It is important that you develop the practice of letting others help you while you are going through your divorce. Chances are that you will make great progress in just a couple of hours with a friend helping you.

Break it down into smaller tasks. If you answer just a few questions a day, the job will not be so overwhelming.

Call your lawyer. Ask whether a paralegal in the office can help you organize the needed information or determine whether some of it can be provided at a later date. A paralegal or associate attorney may be available to meet with you and review the interrogatories so that you can better understand the questions and the information or documentation the opposing party is seeking.

Delay in the discovery process often leads to frustration by clients and lawyers. Do your best to provide the information in a timely manner with the help of others.

5.5 I don't have access to my documents and my spouse is being uncooperative in providing my lawyer with information. Can my lawyer request information directly from an employer or financial institution?

Yes, it may be possible to issue a subpoena directly to an employer or financial institution. A *subpoena* is a court order directing an individual or corporate representative to appear before the court or to produce documents in a pending lawsuit. In the discovery process, a subpoena is used to compel an individual or corporation to produce documents, papers, books, or other physical exhibits that constitute or contain evidence that is relevant to your case.

5.6 My spouse's lawyer intends to subpoena my medical records. Aren't these private?

Whether your medical records are relevant in your case will depend upon the issues in dispute. If you are requesting alimony or if your health is an issue in the dispute of child custody, these records may be relevant. If the records are relevant to the case, your spouse's lawyer may be allowed to review the records.

Talk with your lawyer about your rights. There are a number of options that may be available to prevent or limit the disclosure of your information.

5.7 I own my business. Will I have to disclose my business records?

Yes, you may be required to provide extensive records of your business in the discovery process. However, it is common for the court to protect the confidentiality of these records.

5.8 It's been two months since my lawyer sent interrogatories to my spouse, and we still don't have his answers. I answered mine on time. Is there anything that can be done to speed up the process?

The failure or refusal of a spouse to follow the rules of discovery can add to both the frustration and expense of the divorce process. Talk with your attorney about filing a *motion to compel,* seeking a court order that your spouse provides the requested information by a certain date. A request for attorney fees for the filing of the motion may also be appropriate.

Ask your lawyer whether a subpoena of information from an employer or a financial institution would be a more cost-effective way to get needed facts and documents if your spouse remains uncooperative.

5.9 What is a *deposition*?

A *deposition* is the asking and answering of questions under oath, outside court, in the presence of a court reporter. A deposition may be taken of you, your spouse, or potential witnesses in your divorce case, including experts. Both attorneys will be present. You and your spouse also have the right to be present during the taking of depositions of any witnesses in your case.

Depositions are not performed in every divorce. They are most common in cases involving contested custody, complex financial issues, and expert witnesses.

After your deposition is completed, the questions and answers will be transcribed, that is, typed by the court reporter exactly as given, and then bound into one or more volumes.

5.10 What is the purpose of a deposition?

A deposition can serve a number of purposes such as:

- Supporting the settlement process by providing valuable information
- Helping your attorney determine who to use as witnesses at trial
- Aiding in the assessment of a witness's credibility, that is, whether the witness appears to be telling the truth
- Helping avoid surprises at the trial by learning the testimony of witnesses in advance
- Preserving testimony in the event the witness becomes unavailable for trial

Depositions can be essential tools in a divorce, especially when a case is likely to proceed to trial.

5.11 Will what I say in my deposition be used against me when we go to court?

Usually, a deposition is used to develop trial strategy and obtain information in preparation for trial. In some circumstances, a deposition may be used at trial.

If you are called later to testify as a witness and you give testimony contrary to your deposition, your deposition can be used to impeach you by showing the inconsistency in your statements. This could cause you to lose credibility with the court, rendering your testimony less valuable. It is important to review your deposition prior to your live testimony to ensure consistency and prepare yourself for the type of questions you may be asked.

5.12 Will the judge read the depositions?

Unless a witness becomes unavailable for trial or gives conflicting testimony at trial, it is unlikely that the judge will ever read the depositions.

5.13 How should I prepare for my deposition?

To prepare for your deposition, review the important documents in your case, such as the complaint, your answers to interrogatories, your financial statement, and any other important course pleadings or documents.

Gather any documents you've been asked to provide at your deposition. Deliver them to your attorney in advance of your deposition for copying and review. Talk to your attorney about the type of questions you can expect to be asked. Discuss with him or her any questions you are concerned about answering.

5.14 What will I be asked? Can I refuse to answer questions?

Questions in a deposition can cover a broad range of topics including your education, work, income, and family. The attorney is allowed to ask anything that is reasonably calculated to lead to the discovery of admissible evidence. If the question may lead to relevant information, it can be asked in a deposition, even though it may be inadmissible at trial. If you are unsure whether to answer a question, ask your lawyer and follow his or her advice.

Your attorney may object to inappropriate questions. If there is an objection, say nothing until the attorneys discuss the objection. You will be directed whether or not to answer.

5.15 What if I give incorrect information in my deposition?

You will be under oath during your deposition, so it is very important that you be truthful. If you give incorrect information by mistake, contact your attorney as soon as you realize the error. If you lie during your deposition, you are committing perjury, or lying under oath, which is punishable in the most severe circumstances by criminal prosecution. Even if criminal prosecution is not appropriate, you risk being impeached by the other lawyer during your divorce trial, which could cause you to lose credibility with the court, rendering your testimony less valuable.

5.16 What if I don't know or can't remember the answer to a question?

You may be asked questions about which you have no knowledge. It is always acceptable to say "I don't know" if you do not have the knowledge. Similarly, if you cannot remember, simply say so.

5.17 What else do I need to know about having my deposition taken?

The following suggestions will help you to give a successful deposition:

- Prepare for your deposition by reviewing and providing necessary documents and talking with your lawyer.
- Get a good night's sleep the night before. Eat a meal with protein to sustain your energy, as the length of depositions can vary.
- Arrive early for your deposition so that you have time to get comfortable with your surroundings.
- Relax. You are going to be asked questions about matters you're familiar with. Your deposition is likely to begin with routine matters such as your educational and work history.

- Tell the truth, including whether you have met with an attorney or discussed preparation for the deposition.

- Stay calm. Your spouse's lawyer will be judging your credibility and demeanor. Do not argue with the attorneys.

- Listen carefully to the entire question. Do not try to anticipate questions or start thinking about your answer before the attorney has finished asking the question.

- Answer the question directly. If the question calls only for "yes" or "no," provide such an answer.

- Do not volunteer information. If the lawyer wants to elicit more information, he or she will do so in following questions.

- If you do not understand the question clearly, ask that it be repeated or rephrased. Do not try to answer what you *think* was asked.

- Take your time and carefully consider the question before answering. There is no need to hurry.

- If you do not know or cannot remember the answer, say so. That is an adequate answer.

- Do not guess. If your answer is an estimate or approximation, say so. Do not let an attorney pin you down to anything you are not sure about. For example, if you cannot remember the number of times an event occurred, say that. If the attorney asks you if it was more than ten times, answer only if you can. If you can provide a range (more than ten but less than twenty) with reasonable certainty, you may do so.

- If an attorney mischaracterizes something you said earlier, say so.

- Speak clearly and loudly enough for everyone to hear you.

- Answer all questions with words, rather than gestures or sounds. "Uh-huh" is difficult for the court reporter to distinguish from "unh-unh" and may result in inaccuracies in the transcript.

- If you need a break at any point in the deposition, you have the right to request one. You can talk to your attorney during such a break.

- Discuss with your lawyer in advance of your deposition whether you should review the transcript of your deposition for its accuracy or whether you should waive your right to review and sign the deposition.

Remember that the purpose of your deposition is to support a good outcome in your case. Completing it will help your case to move forward.

5.18 Are depositions always necessary? Does every witness have to be deposed?

Depositions are less likely to be needed if you and your spouse are reaching agreement on most of the facts in your case and you are moving toward a settlement. They are more likely to be needed in cases where child custody is disputed or where there are complex financial issues. Although depositions of all witnesses are usually unnecessary, it is common to take depositions of expert witnesses.

5.19 Will I get a copy of the depositions in my case?

Ask your attorney for a copy of the your deposition. It will be important for you to carefully review your deposition if your case proceeds to trial.

6

Mediation, Arbitration, and Collaboration

If your marriage was full of conflict, you might be asking how you can make the fighting stop. You picture your divorce as having vicious lawyers, an angry spouse, and screaming matches. You wonder if there is any way out of this nightmare.

Or perhaps you and your spouse are parting ways amicably. Although you are in disagreement about how your divorce should be settled, you are clear that you want the process to be respectful and without hostility. You'd rather spend your hard-earned money on your children's college education than legal fees.

In either case, going to trial and having a judge make all of the decisions in your divorce is not inevitable. In fact, most Michigan divorce cases settle without the need for a trial. Mediation and arbitration can help you and your spouse resolve your disputed issues and reach your own agreements without taking your case before the judge who will make your decisions for you.

Resolving your divorce through a mediated or arbitrated settlement has many advantages. You can achieve a mutually satisfying agreement, a known outcome, little risk of appeal, and often enjoy significantly lower legal fees. Despite the circumstances that led to the end of your marriage, it might be possible for your divorce to conclude peacefully with the help of these tools.

Mediation, Arbitration, and Collaboration

6.1 What is the difference between *mediation* and *arbitration*?

Both mediation and arbitration are methods used to help you and your spouse settle your divorce by reaching agreement rather than going to trial and having the judge make decisions for you. These methods are sometimes referred to as *alternative dispute resolution* or *ADR*.

Mediation uses a trained mediator who is an independent, neutral third party. He or she is a skilled professional who can assist you and your spouse in the divorce process. The mediator does not have the authority to order the parties to do anything, or settle the case on specific terms. Rather, the mediator facilitates negotiation between the parties and makes recommendations to resolve the case. *Arbitration* is a similar process, except that the arbitrator's decision is binding and the parties possess limited ability to appeal the decision.

6.2 How are mediation and arbitration different from a collaborative divorce?

Collaborative law is a method of resolving a divorce case where both parties have a strong commitment to settling their disputes and avoiding litigation. You and your spouse each hire an attorney trained in the collaborative law process. You and your lawyers enter into an agreement that provides that in the event either you or your spouse decides to take the case to court both of you must terminate services with your collaborative lawyers and start anew.

Often spouses in the collaborative process enlist the support of other professionals, such as an independent financial advisor or coaches, to support them through the process. Although the process may be lengthy, it enables the focus to shift away from the conflict and toward finding solutions. The attorneys become a part of the team supporting settlement rather than advocates adding to the conflict.

Talk to your lawyer about whether your case would be well suited to the collaborative law process.

6.3   What is involved in the mediation process? What will I have to do, and how long will it take?

The mediation process will be explained to you in detail by the mediator at the start of the mediation session. Mediation involves one or more meetings with you and your attorney, your spouse and his or her attorney, and the mediator. In most mediation sessions, each party and his or her attorney remain in separate rooms and the mediator meets with each party alone to discuss resolution of the case. In some mediation sessions, the mediator will meet with all of the parties together.

The mediator will outline ground rules designed to ensure you will be treated respectfully and given an opportunity to be heard. In most cases, you and your spouse will each be given an opportunity to make some opening remarks about what is important to you in the outcome of your divorce.

How long the process of mediation continues depends upon many of the same factors that affect how long your divorce will take. These include how many issues you and your spouse disagree about, the complexity of these issues, and the willingness of each of you to work toward an agreement.

Your case could settle after just a couple of mediation sessions, or it might require a series of meetings. It is common for the mediator to clarify at the close of each session whether the parties are willing to continue with another session.

6.4   My lawyer said that mediation and arbitration can reduce delays in completing my divorce. How can they accomplish this?

When the issues in your divorce are decided by a judge instead of by you and your spouse, there are many opportunities for delay. These can include:

- Waiting for the trial date
- Having to return to court on a later, second date if your trial is not completed on the day it is scheduled
- Waiting for the judge's ruling on your case
- Needing additional court hearings after your trial to resolve disputes about the intention of your judge's rulings, issues that were overlooked, or disagreement regarding the language of the decree

Each one of these events holds the possibility of delaying your divorce by days, weeks, or even months. Mediating or negotiating the terms of your divorce decree can eliminate these delays.

6.5 How can mediation and negotiation lower the costs of my divorce?

If your case is not settled by agreement, you will be going to trial. If the issues in your case are many or if they are complex, such as custody, the attorney's fees and other costs of going to trial can be tremendous.

By settling your case without going to trial, you may be able to save thousands of dollars in legal fees. Ask your attorney for a litigation budget that sets forth the potential costs of going to trial, so that you have some idea of these costs when deciding whether to settle an issue or to take it to trial before the judge.

6.6 Are there other benefits to mediating a settlement?

Yes. A divorce resolved by a mediated agreement can have these additional benefits:

Recognizing common goals. Mediation allows for brainstorming between the parties and lawyers. Looking at all possible solutions, even the impractical ones, invites creative solutions to common goals. For example, suppose you and your spouse both agree that you need to pay your spouse some amount of equity for the family home you will keep, but you have no cash to make the payment. Together, you might come up with a number of options for accomplishing your goal and select the best one. Contrast this with the judge simply ordering you to pay the money without considering all of the possible options.

Addressing the unique circumstances of your situation. Rather than using a one-size-fits-all approach as a judge might do, a settlement reached by agreement allows you and your spouse to consider the unique circumstances of your situation in formulating a good outcome. For example, suppose you disagree about the parenting times for the Thanksgiving holiday. The judge might order you to alternate the holiday each year, even though you both would have preferred to have your child share the day.

Creating a safe place for communication. Mediation gives each party an opportunity to be heard. Perhaps you and your spouse have not yet had an opportunity to share directly your concerns about settlement. For example, you might be worried about how the temporary parenting time arrangement is impacting your children, but have not yet talked to your spouse about it. A mediation session can be a safe place for you and your spouse to communicate your concerns about your children or your finances.

Fulfilling your children's needs. You may see that your children would be better served by you and your spouse deciding their future rather than having it decided by a judge who does not know, love, and understand your children like the two of you do.

Eliminating the risk and uncertainty of trial. If a judge decides the outcome of your divorce, you give up control over the terms of the settlement. The decisions are left in the hands of the judge. If you and your spouse reach agreement, however, you have the power to eliminate the risk of an uncertain outcome.

Reducing the risk of harm to your children. If your case goes to trial, it is likely that you and your spouse will give testimony that will be upsetting to each other. As the conflict increases, the relationship between you and your spouse inevitably deteriorates. This can be harmful to your children. Contrast this with mediation, in which you open your communication and seek to reach agreement. It is not unusual for the relationship between the parents to improve as the professionals create a safe environment for rebuilding communication and reaching agreements in the best interests of their children.

Having the support of professionals. Using trained professionals, such as mediators and lawyers, to support you can help you to reach a settlement that you might think is impossible. These professionals have skills to help you focus on what is most important to you and shift your attention away from irrelevant facts. They understand the law and know the possible outcomes if your case goes to trial.

Lowering stress. The process of preparing for and going to court can be stressful. Your energy is also going toward caring for your children, looking at your finances, and coping with the emotions of divorce. You might decide that you would be better served by settling your case rather than proceeding to trial.

Achieving closure. When you are going through a divorce, the process can feel as though it is taking an eternity. By reaching agreement, you and your spouse are better able to put the divorce behind you and move forward with your lives.

6.7   Is mediation mandatory?

Yes, in some cases. Although mediation is not mandatory prior to filing for divorce in Michigan, mediation is mandatory in many counties after a divorce filing if you have minor children. Mediation is required to develop a plan for the children, such as custody and parenting time. However, talk to your attorney if you and your spouse have reached an agreement regarding your children because it may be possible to waive the mediation requirement.

6.8   My spouse abused me and I am afraid to participate in mediation. Should I participate anyway?

If you have been a victim of domestic violence by your spouse, it is important that you discuss the appropriateness of mediation with your attorney. Mediation may not be a safe way for you to reach agreement.

Prior to allowing mediation to proceed, any mediator should ask you whether you have been a victim of domestic violence. This is critical for the mediator to both assess your safety and to ensure that the balance of power in the mediation process is maintained.

Talk with your attorney if you have experienced domestic violence or if you feel threatened or intimidated by your spouse. If so, your case may be referred to an approved specialized mediator for parents involved in high-conflict situations. It will be critical to mediate with you and your spouse in different rooms or during separate sessions.

If you do participate in mediation, insist that your mediator have a good understanding of the dynamics of domestic abuse and how they can impact the mediation process.

6.9   What training and credentials do mediators have?

The background of mediators varies. Some are attorneys; many come from other backgrounds such as counseling. Some mediators have received their training through the State of Michigan. Ask your attorney for help in finding a qualified mediator who has experience mediating family law cases. The availability of mediators also varies depending upon where you live. Regional mediation centers are located throughout Michigan.

6.10   What types of issues can be mediated or negotiated?

All of the issues in your case can be mediated. You may decide that certain issues are nonnegotiable for you. Discuss this with your attorney in advance of any mediation sessions so that he or she can support you in focusing the discussions on the issues you are open to looking at.

6.11   What is the role of my attorney in the mediation process?

The role of your attorney in the mediation process will vary depending upon your situation. In some circumstances, your attorney will allow you to speak candidly with the mediator for yourself, especially if you and your spouse remain in separate rooms during mediation. During the discussion of certain issues at mediation, it may be necessary to allow your attorney to speak on your behalf, especially if the discussion involves the law applicable to the issues in your case.

In all cases it is important that your attorney review any agreements discussed in mediation before a final agreement is reached.

6.12   How do I prepare for mediation?

Prior to attending a mediation session with your spouse, discuss with your attorney your strategy and the possible outcomes for resolution of your case.

Make a list of the issues important to you. Giving thought to your desired outcomes while approaching mediation with an open mind and heart is the best way to move closer to settlement.

6.13 Do children attend the mediation sessions?

In most cases your child will not participate in the mediation. If a parenting coordinator or guardian *ad litem* is appointed by the court or enlisted by the parties, the parenting coordinator or guardian *ad litem* may meet with the children and report to the mediator and the parties as to their concerns and/or preferences with respect to custody and parenting time.

6.14 Who pays for mediation?

The cost of mediation must be paid for by you or your spouse. Often it is a shared expense. Expect your mediator to address the matter of fees before or at your first session.

6.15 What if mediation fails?

Either all of the issues are resolved at mediation, or there is no agreement. If mediation is not successful, you still may be able to settle your case through negotiations between the attorneys.

6.16 Why is my lawyer appearing so friendly with my spouse and her lawyer?

Successful negotiations rely upon building trust between the parties working toward agreement. Your lawyer may be respectful or pleasant toward your spouse or your spouse's lawyer to promote a good outcome for you.

6.17 If my spouse and I reach an agreement, how long will it take before it can be finalized?

If a settlement is reached through negotiation or mediation, one of the attorneys will put the agreement in writing for approval by you and your spouse. If you or your spouse request a final hearing and the sixty-day waiting period has expired, in most cases, a final hearing is held within days of the agreement being signed.

7

Emergency:
When You Fear Your Spouse

Suddenly, you are in a panic. Maybe your spouse was serious when threatening to take your child and leave the state. What if you're kicked out of your own home?

Suppose all of the bank accounts are emptied? Your fear heightens as your mind spins with every horror story you've ever heard about divorce.

Facing an emergency situation in divorce can feel as though your entire life is at stake. You may not be able to concentrate on anything else. At the same time, you may be paralyzed with anxiety and have no idea how to begin to protect yourself. No doubt you have countless worries about what your future holds.

Remember that you have overcome many challenges in your life before this moment. There are people willing to help you. You have strength and wisdom you may not yet even realize. Step by step, you will make it through this time.

When facing an emergency, do your best to focus on what to do in the immediate moment. Set aside your worries about the future for another day. Now it is time to stay in the present moment, let others support you, and start taking action right away.

7.1   My spouse has deserted me, and I need to get divorced as quickly as possible. What is my first step?

Your first step is to seek legal advice at your earliest opportunity. The earlier you get legal counsel to advise you about your rights, the better. The initial consultation will answer most of your questions and start you on an action plan for getting your divorce underway.

7.2   I'm afraid my abusive spouse will try to hurt me and/ or our children if I say I want a divorce. What can I do legally to protect myself and my children?

Develop a plan with your safety and that of your children as your highest priority. In addition to meeting with an attorney at your first opportunity, develop a safety plan in the event you and your children need to escape your home. A great way to do this is to let in support from an agency that helps victims of domestic violence. To obtain more information about the domestic violence program closest to you, call the National Domestic Violence Hotline at (800) 799-SAFE (7223) or access the Michigan's Department of Human Services Domestic Violence Resource Directory at www.michigan.gov and search for resources by county.

Your risk of harm from an abusive spouse increases when you leave. For this reason, all actions must be taken with safety as the first concern.

Find a lawyer who understands domestic violence. Often your local domestic violence agency can help with a referral. Talk to your lawyer about the concerns for your safety and that of your children. Ask your lawyer about a *personal protection order.* This is a court order that may offer a number of protections, including granting you temporary custody of your children and ordering your spouse to leave the family residence and have no contact with you.

7.3   I am afraid to meet with a lawyer because I am terrified my spouse will find out and get violent. What should I do?

Schedule an initial consultation with an attorney who is experienced in working with domestic violence victims. When you schedule the appointment, let the firm know your situation and instruct the law office not to place any calls to you that you think your spouse might discover. If possible, pay for your consultation in cash.

Consultations with your attorney are confidential. Your lawyer has an ethical duty to not disclose your meeting with anyone outside the law firm. Let your attorney know your concerns so that extra precautions can be taken by the law office in handling your file.

7.4 I want to give my attorney all the information needed so my children and I are safe from my spouse. What does this include?

Provide your attorney with complete information about the history, background, and nature and evidence of your abuse including:

- The types of abuse (for example, physical, sexual, verbal, financial, mental, emotional)
- The dates, time frames, or occasions
- The locations
- Whether you were ever treated medically
- Any police reports made
- E-mails, letters, notes, text messages, or journal entries
- Any photographs taken
- Any witnesses to the abuse or evidence of the abuse
- Any statements made by your spouse admitting the abuse
- Alcohol or drug abuse by your spouse
- The possession of guns or other weapons by your spouse

The better the information you provide to your lawyer, the easier it will be for him or her to make a strong case for the protection of you and your children.

7.5 I'm not ready to hire a lawyer for a divorce, but I am afraid my spouse is going to get violent with my children and me in the meantime. What can I do?

It is possible to seek a protection order from the court without an attorney. It is possible for the judge to order your spouse out of your home, grant you temporary custody of your children, and order your spouse to stay away from you.

7.6. How do I obtain a personal protection order?

The circuit court for your county will have an office at the courthouse where you can obtain a petition for a personal protection order. Fill out the petition with as much detail as possible to the specific types of abuse and incidents of abuse. If necessary, write down all of the relevant information on additional sheets of paper and attach them to the petition. A judge assigned to your case will review your petition for a personal protection order and decide whether to grant the order based upon the statements contained in your petition—and without notice to your spouse—so the more information you provide the judge, the better your chances of obtaining the order.

Talk to your attorney about obtaining a domestic abuse protection order if you are concerned about your safety, your children's safety, or if there has been a history of domestic abuse. If your spouse has attempted to cause, has caused, or has threatened to cause you bodily injury, you may qualify for a domestic abuse protection order. The violation of a domestic abuse protection order is a criminal offense, which can result in immediate arrest.

If you are concerned that your spouse will annoy, threaten, harass, or intimidate you after your divorce complaint is filed, ask your lawyer about a *civil restraining order*. A civil restraining order is a court order that prohibits a person from engaging in behavior that has been restrained by the court. If your spouse violates the restraining order, he or she may be brought before the court for contempt.

Keep in mind that, although any of the orders can initially be obtained without notice to the spouse, there is always a right to a hearing to determine whether a protection order or restraining order should remain in place.

7.7 My spouse has never been violent, but I know she is going to be really angry and upset when the divorce papers are served. Do I need a protection order?

The facts of your case may not warrant a protection order. However, if you are still concerned about your spouse's behavior, ask your attorney about a *temporary restraining order (TRO)* to be delivered to your spouse at the same time as the divorce complaint. This court order directs your spouse not to annoy, threaten, intimidate, or harass you while the divorce is in progress. A temporary restraining order can also order your spouse not to sell or transfer assets until your divorce is completed.

7.8   I'm afraid my spouse is going to take all of the money out of the bank accounts and leave me with nothing. What can I do?

Talk to your attorney immediately. If you are worried about your spouse emptying financial accounts or selling marital assets, it is critical that you take action at once. Your attorney can advise you on your right to take possession of certain assets in order to protect them from being hidden or spent by your spouse.

Ask your lawyer about seeking an *ex-parte order for asset injunction.* This order is granted on an *ex parte* basis, meaning without notice to your spouse, and forbids your spouse from selling, transferring, hiding, or otherwise disposing of marital property until the divorce is complete. The asset injunction can be served on financial institutions to place them on notice that your spouse may not sell, transfer, or close any assets or accounts under their control.

An asset injunction is intended to prevent assets from "disappearing" before a final division of the property from your marriage is complete. If this is a concern, talk to your lawyer about the benefits of obtaining an asset injunction concerning property, prior to giving your spouse notice that you are filing for divorce.

7.9   My spouse says that I am crazy, that I am a liar, and that no judge will ever believe me if I tell the truth about the abusive behavior. What can I do if I don't have any proof?

Most domestic violence is not witnessed by third parties and judges know this. Often there is little physical evidence. Even without physical evidence, a judge can enter orders to protect you and your children if you give truthful testimony about your abuse that the judge finds believable. Your own testimony of your abuse is evidence.

It is very common for persons who abuse others to claim that their victims are liars and to make statements intended to discourage disclosure of the abuse. This is yet another form of controlling behavior.

Your attorney's skills and experience will support you to give effective testimony in the courtroom to establish your case. Let your lawyer know your concerns so that a strong case can be presented to the judge based upon your persuasive statements of the truth of your experience.

7.10 My spouse told me that if I ever file for divorce, I'll never see my child again. Should I be worried about my child being abducted?

Your fear that your spouse will abduct your child is a common one. It can be helpful to look at some of the factors that appear to increase the risk that your child will be removed from the state by the other parent.

Most abductions are made by men. They are often from marriages that cross culture, race, religion, or ethnicity. A lower socioeconomic status, prior criminal record, and limited social or economic ties to the community can also increase risk.

Programming and brainwashing are almost always present in cases where a child is at risk for being kidnapped by a parent, and efforts to isolate the child may also be seen. Exit activities such as obtaining a new passport, getting financial matters in order, or contacting a moving company could be indicators.

Talk to your lawyer to assess the risks in your particular case. Together you can determine whether statements by your spouse are threats intended to control or intimidate you or whether legal action is needed to protect your child.

7.11 What legal steps can be taken to prevent my spouse from removing our child from the state?

If you are concerned about your child being removed from the state, ask your lawyer whether any of these options might be available in your case:

- A court order giving you immediate custody until a temporary custody hearing can be held

- A court order directing your spouse to turn over passports for the child and your spouse to the court
- The posting of a bond prior to your spouse exercising parenting time
- Supervised visitation

Both state and federal laws are designed to provide protection from the removal of children from one state to another when a custody matter is brought and to protect children from kidnapping. The *Uniform Child Custody Jurisdiction and Enforcement Act (UCCJEA)* was passed to encourage the custody of children to be decided in the state where they have been living most recently and where they have the most ties. The *Parental Kidnapping Prevention Act (PKPA)* makes it a federal crime for a parent to kidnap a child in violation of a valid custody order.

If you are concerned about your child being abducted, talk with your lawyer about all options available to you for your child's protection.

7.12   How quickly can I get a divorce in Michigan?

There are a number of time requirements for getting a divorce in Michigan. Either you or your spouse must have been a resident of Michigan for 180 days immediately prior to the filing of the complaint for the divorce with the court. After you file for divorce, your spouse must be given notice of the divorce.

A sixty-day waiting period is required for every Michigan divorce. This period begins on the date the complaint for divorce is filed. In a divorce matter with minor children, the court imposes a six-month waiting period before a divorce will be granted. However, in some cases the court will waive the six-month waiting period.

The earliest your case can be resolved is after the sixty-day waiting period has expired, although most cases do not resolve this quickly. The length of time your case remains pending depends in large part upon the extent to which you and your spouse reach agreement on the issues in your case.

Your divorce becomes final for most purposes on the date upon which the judge signs your divorce decree.

7.13   I really need a divorce quickly. Will the divorce I get in another country be valid in Michigan?

If both you and your spouse regard Michigan as your true home and you both intend to remain in the state, a divorce from another state or country will not be valid. If Michigan is the permanent home for both of you, you cannot obtain a divorce in another state or country, even if you reside there temporarily.

7.14   If either my spouse or I file for divorce, will I be ordered out of my home? Who decides who gets to live in the house while we go through the divorce?

If you and your spouse cannot reach an agreement regarding which of you will leave the residence during the divorce, the judge will decide whether one of you should be granted exclusive possession of the home until the case is concluded. However, in most cases, judges will refuse to order either party out of the house until the divorce is concluded, absent abusive behavior of one spouse toward the other or the children.

8

Child Custody

Ever since you and your spouse began talking about divorce, chances are your children have been your greatest concern. You or your spouse might have postponed the decision to seek divorce because of concern about the impact on your children. Now that the time has come, you might still have doubts about whether your children will be all right after the divorce.

Remember that you have been making wise and loving decisions for your children since they were born. You've always done your best to see that they had everything they really needed. You loved them and protected them. This won't change because you are going through your divorce. You were a good parent before the divorce, and you will be a good parent after the divorce.

It can be difficult not to worry about how the sharing of parenting time with your spouse will affect your children. You may also have fears about being cut out of your child's life. Try to remember that, regardless of who has custody, it is likely that the court order will not only give you a lot of time with your children but also a generous opportunity to be involved in their day-to-day lives.

With the help of your lawyer, you can make sound decisions regarding the custody arrangement that is in the best interests of your children.

Child Custody

8.1   What types of custody are awarded in Michigan?

Under Michigan law, there are two aspects to a custody determination: legal and physical custody. There can be sole legal custody, joint legal custody, and physical custody. *Legal custody* refers to the power to make fundamental decisions regarding your children, such as which school they attend, what religion they should be brought up in, and who their health care providers are.

Legal custody may be awarded to you, to your spouse, or to both of you jointly. If you have *sole legal custody,* you are the primary and final decision maker for the fundamental decisions regarding your children. *Joint legal custody* means that you and your former spouse will share equally in the fundamental decision making for your child. If you and the other parent are unable to reach agreement, you may need to return to mediation or to court for the decision to be made.

Physical custody refers to the physical location of the children, that is, where they spend their time. Like legal custody, it may be awarded to either parent or to both parents jointly. *Joint physical custody* is sometimes referred to as *shared physical custody.* Notwithstanding who has legal custody, the parent who is with the children will make the day-to-day decisions regarding their care. If you are considering joint physical custody, be sure to discuss with your attorney what is in the best interests of your children.

Specific parenting time will be awarded to each parent, regardless of who has physical custody. Provisions for days of the week, school breaks, summer, holidays, and vacations are typically made in detail. The calculation for child support is based upon the number of overnights the children spend with each parent.

8.2   On what basis will the judge award custody?

The judge considers many factors in determining child custody. Most important is "the best interests of the child." To determine best interests, the judge may look at the following factors:

- The love, affection, and other emotional ties existing between the parties involved and the child

- The capacity and disposition of the parties involved to give the child love, affection, and guidance and to continue the education and raising of the child in his or her religion or creed, if any
- The capacity and disposition of the parties involved to provide the child with food, clothing, medical care, or other remedial care recognized and permitted under the laws of this state in place of medical care, and other material needs
- The length of time the child has lived in a stable, satisfactory environment, and the desirability of maintaining continuity
- The permanence, as a family unit, of the existing or proposed custodial home or homes
- The moral fitness of the parties involved
- The mental and physical health of the parties involved
- The home, school, and community record of the child
- The reasonable preference of the child, if the court considers the child to be of sufficient age to express preference
- The willingness and ability of each of the parties to facilitate and encourage a close and continuing parent-child relationship between the child and the other parent or the child and the parents
- Domestic violence, regardless of whether the violence was directed against or witnessed by the child
- Any other factor considered by the court to be relevant to a particular child-custody dispute

8.3 What's the difference between *visitation* and *parenting time*?

Historically, time spent with the noncustodial parent was referred to as *visitation*. Today, the term *parenting time* is used to refer to the time a child spends with either parent.

This change in language reflects the intention that children spend time with both parents and have two homes, as opposed to their living with one parent and visiting the other.

8.4 How can I make sure I will get to keep the children during the divorce proceedings?

You cannot ensure that your children will stay with you during the divorce process. However, the best way to provide clarity about the living arrangements and respective parenting time with your children during your divorce is to obtain a temporary order. Informal agreements between parties cannot always be trusted. Additionally, informal agreements with your spouse lack the ability to be enforced by the court. Thus, even if you and your spouse have agreed to temporary arrangements, talk with your attorney about whether this agreement should be formalized in a court order.

Obtaining a temporary order can be an important protection not only for the custody of your children, but also for other issues such as support, temporary exclusive possession of the marital home, temporary protection from your spouse, or attorney's fees.

Until a temporary order is entered, it's best that you continue to reside with your children. If you are considering leaving your home, talk with your attorney before making any significant changes to your living situation. If you must leave your home, take your children with you and talk with your attorney at your earliest opportunity.

8.5 How much weight does the child's preference carry?

The preference of your child is only one of many factors a judge may consider in determining custody. The age of your child and his or her ability to express the underlying reason for the preference to live with either parent will determine the amount of weight the judge will give to your child's preference. Although there is no age at which your child's preference determines custody, most judges give more weight to the wishes of an older child.

The reasoning underlying your child's preference is also a factor to consider. Consider the fifteen-year-old girl who wants to live with her mother because "Mom lets me stay out past curfew, I get a bigger allowance, and I don't have to do chores." Greater weight might be given to the preference of an eight-year-old who wants to live with his mother because "She helps me with my homework, reads me bedtime stories, and doesn't call me names like Dad does."

If you see that your child's preference may be a factor in the determination of custody, discuss it with your lawyer so that this consideration is a part of assessing the action to be taken in your case.

8.6 How old do the children have to be before they can speak to the judge about with whom they want to live?

It depends upon the judge. There is no set age at which children are allowed to speak to the judge about their preferences as to custody.

If either you or your spouse wants the judge to listen to what your child has to say, a request is ordinarily made to the judge to have the child speak to the judge *in camera,* meaning in the judge's office (also called the judge's *chambers*) rather than from the witness stand. Depending upon the judge's decision, the attorneys for you and your spouse may also be present.

It is possible that the judge may also allow the attorneys to question the child. If you have concerns about the other parent learning what your child says to the judge, talk to your lawyer about the possibility of obtaining a directive from the court to keep this information confidential.

Typically, the testimony of the child is made *on the record,* that is, in the presence of a court reporter. This is so the testimony can be transcribed later in the event of an appeal.

In addition to the age of a child, a judge may consider such facts as the child's maturity and personality in determining whether an interview of the child by the judge will be helpful to the custody decision-making process.

8.7 How can I prove that I was the primary care provider?

One tool to assist you and your attorney in establishing your case as a primary care provider is a chart indicating the care you and your spouse have each provided for your child. The clearer you are about the history of parenting, the better job your attorney can do in presenting your case to the judge.

Child Custody

Look at the activities in this chart to help you review the role of you and your spouse as care providers for your child.

Parental Roles Chart

Activity	Mother	Father
Attended prenatal medical visits		
Attended prenatal class		
Took time off work after child was born		
Got up with child for feedings		
Got up with child when sick at night		
Bathed child		
Put child to sleep		
Potty-trained child		
Prepared and fed meals to child		
Helped child learn numbers, letters, colors		
Helped child with practice for sports, dance, music		
Took time off work for child's appointments		
Stayed home from work with sick child		
Took child to doctor visits		
Went to pharmacy for child's medication		
Administered child's medication		
Took child to therapy		
Took child to optometrist		
Took child to dentist		
Took child to get haircuts		
Bought clothing for child		
Bought school supplies for child		
Transported child to school		
Picked child up after school		
Drove carpool for child's school		

Parental Roles Chart   (Continued)

Activity	Mother	Father
Went to child's school activities		
Helped child with homework and projects		
Attended parent–teacher conferences		
Helped in child's classroom		
Chaperoned child's school trips and activities		
Transported child to child care		
Communicated with child-care providers		
Transported child from child care		
Attended child-care activities		
Signed child up for sports, dance, music		
Bought equipment for sports, dance, music		
Transported child to sports, dance, music		
Attended child's sports, dance, music practices		
Attended child's sports, dance, music recitals		
Coached child's sports		
Transported child from sports, dance, music		
Know child's friends and friends' families		
Took child to religious education		
Obtained information and training about special needs of child		
Comforted child during times of emotional upset		

8.8   Do I have to let my spouse see the children before we are actually divorced?

Unless your children are at risk for being harmed by your spouse, your children should maintain regular contact with the other parent.

It is important for children to experience the presence of both parents in their lives, regardless of the separation of the parents. Even if there is no temporary order for parenting

88

time, cooperate with your spouse in making reasonable arrangements for time with your children.

When safety is not an issue, if you deny contact with the other parent prior to trial, the judge is likely to question whether you have the best interests of your child at heart. Talk to your spouse or your lawyer about what parenting time schedule would be best for your children on a temporary basis.

8.9 I am seeing a therapist. Will that hurt my chances of getting custody?

If you are seeing a therapist, acknowledge yourself for getting the professional support you need. Your well-being is important to your ability to be the best parent you can be.

Discuss with your lawyer the implications of your being treated by a therapist. It may be that the condition for which you are being treated in no way affects your child or your ability to be a loving and supportive parent.

Your mental health records may be subpoenaed by the other parent's lawyer. For this reason it is important to discuss with your attorney an action plan for responding to a request to obtain records in your therapist's file. Ask your attorney to contact your therapist to alert him or her regarding how to respond to a request for your mental health records.

8.10 I am taking prescription medication to treat my depression. Will this hurt my chances of getting custody?

No. Feelings of depression, anxiety, and trouble sleeping are common during a divorce. If you have any mental health concerns, seek help from a professional. Following through with the recommendations made by your health care provider, including the use of prescription medication, will be looked favorably upon by the court.

8.11 Will my children be present if we go to court?

In most instances, no. Judges make every effort to protect minor children from the conflict of their parents. For this reason, most judges will not allow children to be present in the courtroom to hear the testimony of other witnesses.

Although the risk that your spouse may share information with your child cannot be eliminated, it would be highly unusual for a judge to allow a child to hear such testimony in a courtroom.

8.12 Should I hire a private detective to prove my spouse is having an affair?

If custody is disputed and your spouse is having an affair, discuss with your attorney how a private investigator might help you gather evidence to support your case. Discuss the following considerations with your attorney:

- How is the affair affecting the children?
- How much will a private investigator cost?
- Will the evidence gathered help my case?

Your attorney can help you determine whether hiring a private investigator is a good idea in your particular case.

8.13 Will the fact that I had an affair during the marriage hurt my chances of getting custody?

The concept of fault in the breakdown of the marriage can be considered in determining custody. Therefore, if your spouse alleges that the affair is the reason for the divorce, it may be considered in the custody decision depending upon many factors, including:

- Whether the children were exposed to the affair
- Whether the affair had any impact on the children
- How long ago the affair occurred
- The quality of the evidence about the affair

In determining custody, a court may consider the parent's moral fitness, which includes his or her sexual activity. However, these considerations will be only taken into account if the children were exposed to sexual activity or were adversely affected by the exposure to an affair. This is only one factor the court will consider in making a custody determination. If you had an affair during your marriage, discuss it with your attorney at the outset so that you can assess its impact, if any, on custody.

8.14 During the months it takes to get a divorce, is it okay to date or will it hurt my chances at custody?

If custody is disputed, talk with your attorney about your plans to begin dating. Your dating may be irrelevant if the children are unaware of it. However, most judges will frown upon exposing your children to a new relationship when they are still adjusting to the separation of their parents.

If your spouse is contesting custody, it may be best to focus your energy on your children, the litigation, and taking care of yourself.

If you do date and become sexually involved with your new partner, it is imperative that your children not be exposed to any sexual activity. If they are, it could harm your case for custody.

8.15 Can having a live-in partner hurt my chances of getting custody?

If you are contemplating having your partner live with you, discuss your decision with your attorney first. If you are already living with your partner, let your attorney know right away so that the potential impact on any custody ruling can be assessed.

Your living with someone who is not your spouse may have significant impact on your custody case. However, judges' opinions of the significance of this factor can vary greatly. Talk promptly and frankly with your lawyer. It will be important for you to look together at many aspects, including the following:

- How the judge assigned to your case views this situation
- Whether your living arrangement is likely to prompt a custody dispute that would not otherwise arise
- How long you have been separated from the parent
- How long you have been in a relationship with your new partner
- The history and nature of the children's relationship with your partner
- Your future plans with your partner (such as marriage)

Living with a partner may put your custody case at risk. Consider such a decision thoughtfully, taking account the advice of your lawyer.

8.16 I'm gay and came out to my spouse when I filed for divorce. What impact will my sexual orientation have on my case for custody or parenting time?

There are no laws in Michigan that limit your rights as a parent based upon your sexual orientation. Sexual activity by a parent, whether heterosexual or homosexual, is an insignificant factor in determining custody. However, exposing your child to sexual activity or engaging in sexual activity that harms your child are relevant factors in a custody dispute.

Your sexual orientation is not the same as your sexual activity. Be sure to choose a lawyer you are confident will fully support you in your goals as a parent. Understand that to dispel certain myths, you may need to educate your spouse, opposing counsel, and the judge.

8.17 How is *abandonment* legally defined, and how might it affect the outcome of our custody battle?

Abandonment is rarely an issue in custody litigation unless one parent has been absent from the child's life for an extended period. Under Michigan law, abandonment is determined by the facts and circumstances of each case.

Where abandonment has occurred for a period of more than two years, a court may consider terminating parental rights, but only if doing so would be in the best interests of the child.

8.18 Can I have witnesses speak on my behalf to try to get custody of my children?

Absolutely. Witnesses are critical in every custody case. At a temporary hearing, a witness is more likely to provide testimony by affidavit, which is a written, sworn statement. However, at a trial for the final determination of custody, you and the other parent will each have an opportunity to have witnesses give live testimony on your behalf.

Among those you might consider as potential witnesses in your custody case are:

- Family members
- Family friends
- Child-care providers
- Neighbors
- Teachers
- Health care providers
- Clergy members

In considering which witnesses would best support your case, your attorney may consider the following:

- What has been this witness's opportunity to observe you or the other parent, especially with your child?
- How frequently? How recently?
- How long has the witness known you or the other parent?
- What is the relationship of the witness to the child and the parents?
- How valuable is the knowledge that this witness has?
- Does this witness have knowledge different from that of other witnesses?
- Is the witness available and willing to testify?
- Is the witness clear in conveying information?
- Is the witness credible, that is, will the judge believe this witness?
- Does the witness have any biases or prejudices that could impact the testimony?

You and your attorney can work together to determine which witnesses will best support your case. Support your attorney by providing a list of potential witnesses together with your opinion regarding the answers to the above questions.

Give your attorney the phone numbers, addresses, and workplaces of each of your potential witnesses. This information can be critical to the role that the attorney has in interviewing the witnesses, contacting them regarding testifying, and issuing subpoenas to compel their court attendance if needed. When parents give conflicting testimony during a custody trial, the testimony of other witnesses can be key to determining the outcome of the case.

8.19   Will my attorney want to speak with my children?

In most cases your attorney won't ask to speak with your children. An exception might be where custody is disputed or where either parent has made allegations of abuse or neglect. Not all attorneys are trained in appropriate interviewing techniques for children, especially for younger children. If the attorney has not spent a lot of time with children or is not familiar with child development, the interview may not provide meaningful information. Don't hesitate to ask your attorney about his or her experience in working with children before you agree to an interview of your child.

If your attorney asks to meet with your child, provide some background information about your child first. Let your attorney know your child's personality, some of his or her interests, and any topics that might upset your child. This background will help the attorney exercise the care essential any time a professional questions a child.

If you are concerned that going to your attorney's office for an interview will cause undue anxiety for your child, ask your attorney whether the interview can take place in a setting that would be more comfortable for your child. This might be a public place or your home.

8.20   How might photographs or a video of my child help my custody case?

Photographs or a video depicting your child's day-to-day life can help the judge learn more about your child's needs. It can demonstrate how your child interacts with you, siblings, and other important people in your family's life. The photographs or video can portray your child's room, home, and neighborhood, as well as show your child participating in activities.

Talk to your lawyer about whether photographs or a video would be helpful in your case. Although photographs are more commonly used and are typically sufficient evidence, ask your lawyer if he or she recommends making a video, and if so, what scenes to include, the length of the video, keeping the original tapes, and the editing process.

8.21   Who is a guardian *ad litem*? Why is one appointed?

In custody cases, a guardian *ad litem* is an individual who is appointed by the court to represent the best interests of the child. The guardian *ad litem* (sometimes referred to as the *GAL*), typically an attorney, is directed by the judge to conduct an investigation on the issue of custody. Historically, guardians *ad litem* were used for this purpose.

8.22   Why might I not be awarded sole physical custody?

A parent who is awarded sole physical custody has the authority and responsibility regarding the child's place of residence. In determining physical custody and parenting arrangements, the court considers the best interests of the minor child, which include, but are not limited to the following considerations:

- The relationship of the minor child to each parent prior to the commencement of the action or temporary hearing
- The desires and wishes of the minor child, if of an age of comprehension but regardless of chronological age, when such desires and wishes are based on sound reasoning
- The general health, welfare, and social behavior of the minor child
- Credible evidence of abuse inflicted on any family or household member

You may not be awarded sole physical custody if the judge determines that although you are fit to be awarded custody, it is in your child's best interests that custody be awarded to both parents.

Additionally, you may be denied sole physical custody if the judge determines that you are not fit to be a custodial parent.

8.23   What does it mean to be an *unfit* parent?

Parental *unfitness* means that you have a personal deficiency or incapacity that will likely prevent you from performing essential parental obligations and is likely to result in a detriment to your child's well-being.

Determinations of your fitness to be a custodial parent will largely depend upon the facts of your case. Reasons why a parent might be found to be unfit include a history of physical abuse, alcohol or drug abuse, or mental health problems that affect the ability to parent.

8.24 Does joint physical custody always mean equal time at each parent's house?

No. Joint physical custody really only means the parents share parenting time with the child. Joint physical custody does not necessarily require that each parent have equal amounts of parenting time.

8.25 If I am awarded joint physical custody, what are some examples of how the parenting might be shared?

In joint physical custody arrangements, many parents follow a 2-3-2 schedule, or a variation thereof, whereby one parent has the child for two weekdays, the other parent has the child for the following two weekdays, and then the child goes back to the first parent for a three-day weekend. Below is an example parenting chart to demonstrate the 2-3-2 schedule.

	Monday	Tuesday	Wednesday	Thursday	Friday	Saturday	Sunday
Week 1	Mother at 8:00 A.M.	Mother	Father beginning at 5:00 P.M.	Father	Mother beginning at 5:00 P.M.	Mother	Mother
Week 2	Father at 8:00 A.M.	Father	Mother beginning at 5:00 P.M.	Mother	Father beginning at 5:00 P.M.	Father	Father

Some parents prefer to have a one-week-on, one-week-off parenting schedule. However, this is not preferred by the courts because the child is away from the other parent for such an extended period of time.

Often a joint custody parenting time schedule only involves every other weekend and a weekday dinner for one parent. This may not sound like joint custody but it is often preferred by a working parent with a busy schedule. For that reason, it is important not to grow too concerned about the label of "joint physical custody." It is most important to find a parenting time schedule that works well with the daily schedules of the children and the parties.

8.26 How is legal custody decided?

The parent who is awarded legal custody has the responsibility and authority to make all fundamental decisions regarding the child's welfare. Examples of fundamental decisions, include, but are not limited to, issues such as religion, education, and nonemergency medical treatment.

You can be awarded either sole or joint legal custody. If you are awarded sole legal custody, you have the sole authority to make fundamental decisions for your child, such as what school your child will attend, who your child's treating physician will be, and whether your child should undergo elective treatments or surgeries. However, even if you are awarded sole legal custody, your spouse still has the authority and responsibility to make the day-to-day decisions for your child when he or she is in your spouse's care.

It is extremely rare for a judge to award sole legal custody to one party absent a pattern of extremely egregious behavior by the other party, such as domestic violence or severe alcohol or drug abuse. In some situations, if one party can prove that the relationship between the parties is so strained that communication is impossible and they will not be able to agree, the judge may consider awarding legal custody to one party to avoid the constant appearances of the parties in court for resolution of issues.

If you are awarded joint legal custody, you and your spouse will share the decision-making authority. This necessitates that you and your spouse are able to communicate and agree upon fundamental decisions regarding your children. You and your spouse might be good candidates for joint legal custody if you share a mutual respect for each other, you are able to communicate effectively, and you are able to cooperate and work together in a co-parenting relationship.

If you share joint legal custody and are unable to reach agreement on a major decision, such as a child's school or child-care provider, you and your former spouse may be required to return to mediation or to court to resolve your dispute. This can lead to delays in decision making for matters important to your child, increased conflict, and legal fees.

8.27   If my spouse is awarded physical custody of my child, how much time will our child spend with me?

Parenting time schedules for noncustodial parents vary from case to case. However, historically, the standard parenting time schedule for noncustodial parents is alternating weekends and one evening during the week. Additionally, holidays are alternated between the parents and Mother's Day and Father's Day are spent with the appropriate parent. Holiday parenting time supersedes the regular weekly schedule for parenting time.

As in the determination of custody, the best interests of the child are what a court considers in determining the parenting time schedule. Among the factors that can impact a parenting time schedule are the past history of parenting time, the age and needs of the child, and the parents' work schedules.

If you and your spouse are willing to reach your own agreement about the parenting time schedule, you are likely to be more satisfied with it than with one imposed by a judge. Because the two of you know your child's needs, your family traditions, and your personal preferences, you can design a plan uniquely suited to your child's best interests.

If you and your spouse are unable to reach an agreement on a parenting time schedule, either on your own or with the assistance of your lawyers or a mediator, the judge will decide the schedule.

8.28   What does it mean to have *split custody*?

Split custody refers to a custodial arrangement whereby each parent has sole physical custody of one or more of the children. Courts generally disfavor split custody because it separates the children from each other. However, in families with a disabled child, or a child who is in need of additional health services, the use of split custody can provide for more attention and care focused upon the child in need.

8.29 What is a *parenting plan*?

A *parenting plan* is a document detailing how you and your spouse will be parenting your child after the divorce. Among the issues addressed in a parenting plan are:

- Custody, both legal and physical
- Parenting time, including specific times for:
  - Regular school year
  - Holidays
  - Birthdays
  - Mother's Day and Father's Day
  - Summer
  - School breaks
- Phone access to the child
- Communication regarding the child
- Access to records regarding the child
- Notice regarding parenting time
- Attendance at the child's activities
- Decision making regarding the child
- Exchange of information such as addresses, phone numbers, and care providers

Detailed parenting plans are good for children and parents. They increase clarity for the parents, provide security for the child in knowing what to expect, reduce conflict, and lower the risk of needing to return to court for a modification of your divorce decree.

8.30 I don't think it's safe for my children to have any contact with my spouse. How can I prove this to the judge?

Keeping your children safe is so important that this discussion with your attorney requires immediate attention. Talk with your attorney about a plan for the protection of you and your children. Options might include supervised visitation or certain restrictions on your spouse's parenting time, such as no overnight visitation. However, it is rare for the court to enter a no-contact order with respect to children, and the court will not enter a personal protection order by a child against a parent.

Make sure you have an attorney who understands your concerns for the welfare of your children. If your attorney is not taking your worry about the safety of your children seriously, you may be better served by a lawyer with a greater understanding of the issues in your case.

Give your attorney a complete history of the facts upon which you base your belief that your children are not safe with the other parent. Although the most recent facts are often the most relevant, it is important that your attorney have a clear picture of the background as well.

Your attorney also needs information about your spouse, such as whether your spouse is or has been:

- Using alcohol or drugs
- Treated for alcohol or drug use
- Arrested, charged, or convicted of crimes of violence
- In possession of firearms
- Subject to a protection order for harassment or violence

8.31　How can I get my spouse's parenting time to be supervised?

If you are concerned about the safety of your children when they are with your spouse, talk to your lawyer. It may be that a protection order is warranted to terminate or limit contact with your children. Alternatively, it is possible to ask the judge to consider certain court orders intended to better protect your children.

Ask your attorney whether, under the facts of your case, the judge would consider any of the following court orders:

- Supervised visits
- Exchanges of the children in a public place
- Parenting class for the other parent
- Anger management or other rehabilitative program for the other parent
- A prohibition against drinking by the other parent when with the children

Judges have differing approaches to cases where children are at risk. Recognize that there are also often practical considerations, such as cost or the availability of people to supervise visits. Urge your attorney to advocate zealously for court orders to protect your children from harm by the other parent.

8.32 My spouse keeps saying he'll get custody because there were no witnesses to his abuse and I can't prove it. Is he right?

No. Most domestic violence is not witnessed by others, and judges know this.

If you have been a victim of abusive behavior by your spouse, or if you have witnessed your children as victims, your testimony is likely to be the most compelling evidence.

Be sure to tell your attorney about anyone who may have either seen your spouse's behavior or spoken to you or your children right after an abusive incident. They may be important witnesses in your custody case.

8.33 I am concerned about protecting my child from abuse by my spouse. Which types of past abuse by my spouse are important to tell my attorney?

Keeping your child safe is your top priority. So that your attorney can help you protect your child, give him or her a full history of the following:

- Hitting, kicking, pushing, shoving, or slapping your or your child
- Sexual abuse
- Threats to harm you or the child
- Threats to abduct your child
- Destruction of property
- Torture of pets or harm to them
- Requiring your child to keep secrets

The process of writing down past events may help you to remember other incidents of abuse that you had forgotten. Be as complete as possible.

8.34 What documents or items should I give my attorney to help prove the history of domestic violence by my spouse?

The following may be useful exhibits if your case goes to court:

- Photographs of injuries
- Photographs of damaged property
- Abusive or threatening notes, letters, or e-mails
- Abusive or threatening voice messages or text messages
- Your journal entries about abuse
- Police reports
- Medical records
- Court records
- Criminal and traffic records
- Damaged property, such as torn clothing

Tell your attorney which of these you have or are able to obtain. Ask your lawyer whether others can be acquired through a subpoena or other means.

8.35 I want to talk to my spouse about our child, but all she wants to do is argue. How can I communicate without it always turning into a fight?

Because conflict is high between you and your spouse, consider the following:

- Ask your lawyer to help you obtain a court order for custody and parenting time that is specific and detailed. This lowers the amount of necessary communication between you and your spouse.
- Put as much information in writing as possible.
- Consider using e-mail or mail, especially for less urgent communication.
- Avoid criticisms of your spouse's parenting.
- Avoid telling your spouse how to parent.
- Be factual and businesslike.

- Acknowledge to your spouse the good parental qualities he or she displays, such as being concerned, attentive, or generous.
- Keep your child out of any conflicts.

By focusing on your behavior, conflict with your spouse has the potential to decrease. Additionally, talk to your attorney about developing a communication protocol to follow when communicating with your spouse.

8.36   If my child is not returned from parenting time at the agreed-upon time, should I call the police?

Calling the police should be done only as a last resort if you feel that your child is at risk for abuse or neglect, or if you have been advised by your attorney that such a call is warranted. The involvement of law enforcement officials in parental conflict can result in far greater trauma to a child than a late return at the end of a parenting time.

The appropriate response to a child not being returned according to a court order depends upon the circumstances. If the problem is a recurring one, talk to your attorney regarding your options. It may be that a change in the schedule would be in the best interests of your child.

Regardless of the behavior of the other parent, make every effort to keep your child out of any conflicts between the adults.

8.37   If I have sole custody, may I move out of state without the permission of the court?

No. A custodial parent must obtain permission of the court prior to moving more than 100 miles from the current residence of the child. If your former spouse agrees to your move, contact your attorney for preparing and submitting the necessary documents to your former spouse and the court for approval.

If your former spouse objects to your move, you must apply to the court for permission, give your spouse notice of the application, and have a court hearing for the judge to decide.

To obtain the court's permission, you must first prove that you have a legitimate reason for the move, such as a better job or a transfer of your new spouse's employment. You must also prove that the move is in the best interests of your child. Temporary removal of a child in such cases is ordinarily not granted. It may be important to expedite your case so you will have a final court ruling determining whether you may move out of state with your child.

8.38 I am considering moving out of state. What factors will the court consider in either granting or denying my request to remove my child from Michigan?

If you are considering an out-of-state move, talk to your attorney immediately. In order to leave Michigan with your child, you must have a legitimate reason for leaving the state. The court considers four factors before permitting a change of the child's legal residence:

- Whether the change will improve the quality of life for the child and the relocating parent
- How well both parents have utilized their parenting time under the current court order or agreement or whether the move is strictly an attempt to limit the other parent's parenting time
- The ability to modify the parenting time schedule in a way that will allow the other parent to preserve and foster the relationship with the child and whether the parties will comply with the new schedule
- The extent to which the parent opposing the move is seeking a financial advantage with respect to a support obligation (having more overnights simply to pay less support).

Even if you have not finalized your plans to leave Michigan, seek advice from your attorney. He or she can help you gather important information that may be needed in your removal case.

8.39 After the divorce, can my spouse legally take our children out of the state during parenting time? Out of the country?

It depends upon the terms of the court order as set forth in your decree. If you are concerned about your children being out of Michigan with the other parent, you may want some of these decree provisions regarding out-of-state travel with your child:

- Limits on the duration or distance for out-of-state travel with the child
- Notice requirements
- Information on phone numbers
- Information on physical addresses
- E-mail address contact information
- Possession of the child's passport with the court
- Posting of bond by the other parent prior to travel
- Requiring a court order for travel outside the country

Although judges are not ordinarily concerned about short trips across state lines, you should let your attorney know if you are concerned that your child may be abducted by the other parent so that reasonable safeguards may be put in place.

8.40 If I am not given physical custody, what rights do I have regarding medical records and medical treatment for my child?

Regardless of which parent has physical custody, state law allows that if parents have joint legal custody, both parents shall have access to the medical records of their children and the right to make emergency medical decisions. Again, courts award parents joint legal custody the majority of the time, absent a showing that one parent is completely unsuitable—for example, a parent who is abusive, an alcoholic, or extremely incapable of communicating with the other party such that the court has no choice but to award one parent complete decision-making authority.

8.41 If I'm not the primary caregiver, how will I know what's going on at my child's school? What rights to records do I have there?

Regardless of your physical custodial status, if you have joint legal custody you have a right to have access to your child's school records.

Develop a relationship with your child's teachers and the school staff. Request to be put on the school's mailing list for all notices. Find out what is necessary for you to do to get copies of important school information and report cards.

Communicate with the other parent to both share and receive information about your child's progress in school. This will enable you to support your child and each other through any challenging periods of your child's education. It also enables you to share a mutual pride in your child's successes.

Regardless of which parent has custody, your child will benefit by your involvement in his or her education through your participation in parent–teacher conferences, attendance at school events, help with school homework, and positive communication with the other parent.

8.42   If my spouse is awarded legal custody, can I still take my child to church during my parenting time?

Yes. The decision as to which religion the child should be brought up in should be a fundamental decision that is made by the parent who has legal custody. However, a noncustodial parent retains the authority to make day-to-day decisions for the child while he or she is in their care. This means that a noncustodial parent can still take their child to the church of their choice or participate in religious activities of their choice during their parenting time.

8.43   What if my child does not want to go for his or her parenting time? Can my former spouse force the child to go?

If your child is resisting going with the other parent, it can first be helpful to determine the underlying reason. Consider these questions:

- What is your child's stated reason for not wanting to go?
- Does your child appear afraid, anxious, or sad?
- Do you have any concerns regarding your child's safety while with the other parent?
- Have you prepared your child for being with the other parent, speaking about the experience with enthusiasm and encouragement?

- Is it possible your child is perceiving your anxiety about the situation and is consequently having the same reaction?

- Have you provided support for your child's transition to the other home, such as completing fun activities in your home well in advance of the other parent's starting time for parenting?

- Have you spoken to the other parent about your child's behavior?

- Can you provide anything that will make your child's time with the other parent more comfortable, such as a favorite toy or blanket?

- Have you established clear routines that support your child to be ready to go with the other parent with ease, such as packing a backpack or saying good-bye to a family pet?

The reason for a child's reluctance to go with the other parent may be as simple as being sad about leaving you or as serious as being a victim of abuse in the other parent's home. It is important to look at this closely to determine the best response.

Judges treat compliance with court orders for parenting time seriously. If one parent believes that the other is intentionally interfering with parenting time or the parent–child relationship, it can result in further litigation. At the same time, you want to know that your child is safe. Talk with your attorney about the best approach in your situation.

8.44 What steps can I take to prevent my spouse from getting the children in the event of my death?

Unless the other parent is not fit to have custody, he or she will have first priority as the guardian of your child in the event of your death. All parents should have a will naming a guardian for their children. In the event you do not intend to name the other parent, talk with your attorney. Seek counsel about how to best document and preserve the evidence that will be needed to prove that the other parent is unfit to have custody in the event of your death.

9

Child Support

Whether you will be paying or receiving child support is often the subject of much worry. Will you receive enough support to take care of your children? Will you have enough money to live on after you pay child support? How will you make ends meet?

Most parents want to provide for their children. Today, the child-support laws make it possible for parents to have a better understanding of their obligation to support their children. The mechanisms for both payment and receipt of child support are more clearly defined, and help is available for collecting support if it's not paid.

The Michigan Child Support Guidelines, the Michigan Friend of Court, and the Michigan State Disbursement Unit ("MiSDU") all help to simplify the child-support system. As you learn more about them, matters regarding child support that appeared complex in the beginning can eventually become routine for you and the other parent.

9.1   What determines whether I will get child support?

Whether you will receive child support depends upon a number of factors. These may include how much time your child is living in your household, which parent has custody, and each parent's ability to pay support.

If your spouse is not the biological or adoptive parent of your child, it is possible you will not receive child support from your spouse. If paying child support will cause your spouse to reduce his or her net income below the federal poverty guide-line, the support you receive may be as little as $50 per month.

If you have physical custody of your child, it is likely your spouse will be ordered to pay support for any children born or adopted during your marriage.

9.2   Can I request child support even if I do not meet the 180-day residency requirement for a divorce in Michigan?

Yes. Even though you may not have met the requirements to obtain a divorce, you have a right to seek support for your children.

9.3   Can I get temporary support while waiting for custody to be decided?

A judge has authority to enter a temporary order for custody and child support. This order ordinarily remains in place until a final decree establishing custody is entered. In most cases a hearing for temporary custody and support can be held shortly after the filing of the complaint for divorce.

9.4   What is *temporary support*, and how soon can I get it?

Temporary support is the support paid for a spouse or a child. It is paid sometime after the divorce complaint is filed and continues until your final decree of divorce is entered by the court or until your case is dismissed.

If you are in need of temporary support, talk to your attorney about this need at your first opportunity. If you and your spouse are unable to agree upon the amount of temporary support to be paid each month, it is likely that your attorney will file a motion for temporary support asking the judge to decide how much the support should be and when it will start.

Because there are a number of steps to getting a temporary child-support order, don't delay in discussing your need for support with your lawyer. Child support will not be ordered for any period prior to the filing of a request for it with the court. The following are the common steps in the process:

- You discuss your need for temporary child support with your lawyer.

- Your lawyer requests a hearing date from the judge and prepares the necessary documents.
- A temporary hearing is held.
- The temporary order is signed by the judge.
- Your spouse begins paying you support directly or your spouse's employer is notified to begin withholding your support from your spouse's paychecks; this support is then sent to MiSDU, logged in the system, and then sent to you.

If your spouse is not paying you support voluntarily, time is of the essence in obtaining a temporary order for support. This should be one of the first issues you discuss with your lawyer.

9.5 How soon does my spouse have to start paying support for the children?

Your spouse may begin paying you support voluntarily at any time. A temporary order for support will give you the right to collect the support if your spouse stops paying. Talk to your lawyer about court hearings for temporary support in your county. You may have to wait for a week or two before your temporary hearing can be held. It is possible that the judge will not order child support to start until the first of the following month.

9.6 How is the amount of child support I'll receive or pay figured?

The Michigan Child Support Guidelines were created by the Michigan Supreme Court to set forth the standards by which your child support is calculated. According to the guidelines, both parents have a duty to contribute to the support of their children in proportion to their respective net incomes. As a result, both your income and the income of your spouse will factor into the child-support calculation. The formula for the calculation of child support is based upon the needs of the children, the income of the parties, the number of children, and the number of overnights for each parent.

Other factors the court may consider include:
- The additional cost of health insurance for the child
- The child-care costs for the child
- Regularly paid support for other children
- Substantial fluctuations of annual earnings by either parent during the past three years
- Which parent claims the children as exemptions for tax purposes
- Child support that is higher or lower than what the guidelines provide for may be awarded in certain cases, for example:
  - When either parent or child has extraordinary medical costs
  - When a child is disabled with special needs
  - For juveniles placed in foster care
  - Whenever the application of the guidelines in an individual case would be unjust or inappropriate

When a judge orders an amount of support that is different from the guideline amount, it is referred to as a *deviation*.

Due to the complexity of calculations under the guidelines, many attorneys use computer software to calculate child support.

9.7 Will the type of custody arrangement or the amount of parenting time I have impact the amount of child support I receive?

It can. The number of overnights your spouse has with the child can dramatically lower child-support amounts. For this reason, it is essential that you discuss child support with your attorney prior to reaching any agreements with your spouse regarding custody or parenting time.

9.8 Is overtime pay considered in the calculation of child support?

Yes, if your overtime is a routine part of your employment that you can actually expect to earn regularly. The judge can consider your work history, the degree of control you have over your overtime, and the nature of the field in which you work.

9.9   Will rental income be factored into my child support, or just my salary?

Yes. Income from other sources may be considered in determining the amount of child support.

9.10   My spouse has a college degree but refuses to get a job. Will the court consider this in determining the amount of child support?

The earning capacity of your spouse may be considered instead of current income. The court can look at your spouse's work history, education, skills, health, and job opportunities.

If you believe your spouse is earning substantially less than the income she or he is capable of earning, provide your attorney with details. Ask about making a case for child support based on earning capacity instead of actual income.

9.11   Will I get the child support directly from my spouse or from the state?

It depends. Child support can be withheld from the income of the payor of child support. Employers routinely withhold child support from employee wages just as they withhold taxes or retirement.

If the parent's income is not being withheld by his or her employer, the parent either makes child-support payments directly to you or makes child-support payments through the Friend of the Court (FOC) and Michigan State Disbursement Unit (MiSDU). Payments to MiSDU can be made either electronically or by mail. The Payment Center then sends the child support to the parent receiving support via check, debit card, or direct deposit.

Be sure to talk with your attorney about the pros and cons of paying child support through the FOC and MiSDU. The most obvious benefit of receiving payments through the FOC and MiSDU is that MiSDU keeps track of your payments and notes if the parent paying support has failed to make payments. The FOC can initiate a hearing to bring in a parent who has failed to pay to explain why payments are behind and bring payments current or face consequences from the court.

9.12 How will I receive my child-support payment through MiSDU?

The Michigan Child Support Payment Center has several methods of disbursing your child-support money. The Payment Center can send your child-support check in the mail. However, it may take three to five business days for processing through the mail. This time frame may be even longer if it is an out-of-state check or a certified check.

You can also receive your payment by direct deposit so that your child-support payment is automatically deposited into your bank account. Additionally, your child support can be deposited directly onto an electronic payment card, which operates as a debit card. With the electronic payment card, your child-support payments will be transferred electronically into your card account, from which you can access your money at any automated teller machine (ATM), and which is accepted anywhere debit cards are accepted. Receiving your child-support payment by direct deposit or by an electronic payment card is the fastest way to obtain your payments.

More information can be found on the Michigan State Disbursement Unit website at www.misdu.com.

9.13 Is there any reason not to pay or receive payments directly to or from my spouse once the court has entered a child-support order?

Yes. By avoiding direct payments to your former spouse, you and he or she will have accurate records. Once a child-support order is entered by the court, the Michigan Child Support Payment Center keeps a record of all support paid. If a payment is not made, the state's records will show that you are behind in your child support. These state records cannot be kept if payments are made directly from one spouse to the other.

Direct payments of child support can also result in misunderstandings between parents. The payor may have intended the money to pay a child-support payment, but the parent receiving the support may have thought it was extra money to help with the child's expenses. The payment of support through MiSDU protects both parents.

9.14 Can I go to the courthouse to pick up my child-support payment?

All child-support payments in Michigan are processed through a central location at the Michigan State Disbursement Unit in Lansing.

9.15 How soon can I expect my child-support payments to start arriving?

A number of factors may affect the date on which you will begin receiving your child support. Here are the usual steps in the process:

- A child-support amount and start date for the support are decided either by agreement between you and your spouse or by the judge.
- Either your attorney or your spouse's attorney prepares the court order.
- The attorney who did not write the court order reviews and approves it.
- The court order is taken to the judge for signature.
- The FOC generates an Income Withholding Order and sends it to the employer of the party who is paying, asking that child support be withheld from future paychecks.
- Your spouse's employer withholds the support from the paycheck.
- The child support is transferred by the employer to MiSDU.
- MiSDU sends the money to you, either by direct deposit or mail.

As you can see, there are a lot of steps in this process. Plan your budget knowing that the initial payment of child support might be delayed.

9.16 Will some amount of child support be withheld from every paycheck?

It depends upon the employer's policy and how you are paid. If support is due on the first of the month, the employer has the full month to withhold the amount ordered to be paid. If an employer issues paychecks twice a month, it is possible

114

that half of the support will be withheld from each check and paid to MiSDU all at once at the end of the month or twice a month.

If an employer issues checks every other week, which is twenty-six pay periods per year, there will be some months in which a third paycheck is issued. Consequently, it is possible that no child support will be withheld from the wages paid in that third check of the month or that some checks will be for less than 50 percent of the monthly amount due.

Example: Suppose child support is $650 per month. Payor is paid every other Friday, or twenty-six times per year. The employer may withhold $300 per paycheck for child support. Although most months the support received will be $600, for a few months it will be $900. By the end of the year, however, the payor will have paid the same amount as if $650 had been paid each month.

Over time, child-support payments typically fall into a routine schedule, which makes it easier for both the payor and the recipient of support to plan their budgets.

9.17   If my spouse has income other than from an employer, is it still possible to get a court order to withhold my child support from his income?

Yes. Child support can be automatically withheld from most sources of income. These may include unemployment, worker's compensation, retirement plans, employment bonuses, and investment income.

9.18   The person I am divorcing is not the biological parent of my child. Can I still collect child support from my spouse?

Perhaps. Your spouse may be ordered to pay child support under certain circumstances. Among the factors the court will consider is whether your spouse is acting in the role of a parent to your child.

Discuss the facts of your case in detail with your lawyer. When you are clear about what will be in the best interests of your child, your attorney can support you in developing a strategy for your case that takes into consideration not only child support but also the future relationship of your spouse with your child.

9.19 Can I collect child support from both the biological parent and the adoptive parent of my child?

When your child was adopted, the biological parent's duty to support your child ended. However, it may be possible for you to collect past-due child support from the period of time before the adoption.

9.20 What happens with child support when our children go to the other parent's home for summer vacation? Is child support still due?

It depends. Whether child support is adjusted during extended parenting times with the noncustodial parent depends upon the court order in your case. In 2008, the child-support formula eliminated the possibility of an abatement, or reduction, of child support due to extended periods of parenting time with a noncustodial parent.

9.21 What is a *child-support referee*?

Although it is likely that your child support will be decided by the judge hearing your divorce, *child-support referees* are also authorized to hear matters regarding child support and spousal support. Referees are attorneys who work for the Michigan FOC and are appointed to conduct hearings in the same manner as a judge.

After hearing the evidence, the referee will draw conclusions regarding the facts and make recommendations to the judge. The judge then has the authority to enter an order based upon the referee's written report.

If you are dissatisfied with the referee's findings and recommendations, talk to your attorney right away about filing an objection.

9.22 After the divorce, if I choose to live with my new partner rather than marry, can I still collect child support?

Yes. Although spousal support (alimony) may end if you live with your partner, child support does not terminate for this reason.

9.23 Can I still collect child support if I move to another state?

Yes. A move out of state will not end your right to receive child support. However, the amount of child support could be changed if other circumstances change, such as income or costs for exercising parenting time.

9.24 Can I expect to continue to receive child support if I remarry?

Yes. Your child support will continue even if you remarry.

9.25 How long can I expect to receive child support?

Under Michigan law, child support is ordinarily ordered to be paid until the child dies, marries, is emancipated (becomes self-supporting), reaches the age of eighteen, or reaches the age of nineteen and a half while still enrolled in high school.

9.26 Does interest accrue on past-due child support?

No, not interest exactly. The law provides that a surcharge, calculated from the rate (derived from the five-year U.S. treasury note rate), may be added to the arrearage (past-due child support) twice per year, on January 1 and July 1. The court will order a surcharge to be added only if it determines that the payer failed to pay support according to a support order and the failure was willful. The surcharge is added to the total arrearage but does not compound annually.

9.27 What can I do if my former spouse refuses to pay child support?

If your former spouse is not paying child support, you may take action to enforce the court order either with the help of your lawyer or the assistance of the FOC referee assigned to your case. Unlike a private attorney, you do not pay for the services of a referee. Visit the FOC website at www. friendofthecourt.org for the court in your county for a list of frequently asked questions and court forms that will be useful to you in initiating a proceeding with the referee to enforce your support order.

The judge may order payment of both the current amount of support and an additional amount to be paid each month until the past-due child support (arrearages) is paid in full.

You may request that your former spouse's state and federal tax refunds be sent directly to MiSDU. It may also be possible to garnish a checking or savings account.

Driver's licenses may also be suspended if a parent falls behind in child-support payments if the arrearage exceeds an amount equal to two months of periodic payments.

Your former spouse may also be found in *contempt of court* if the failure to pay support is intentional. Possible consequences include being fined or jailed.

To review, if you are not receiving child support, you have two options:

• Call your attorney.

• Contact the Michigan Friend of the Court referee assigned to your case.

If you do not know who the referee assigned to your case is, you can call the county courthouse, ask to speak to the clerk, and provide your case number and the clerk will be able to tell you the name and telephone number of the referee.

9.28 I live outside Michigan. Will the money I spend on airline tickets to see my children impact my child support?

It might. If you expect to spend large sums of money for transportation in order to have parenting time with your children, talk to your attorney about how this might be taken into consideration when determining the amount of child support.

9.29 After the divorce, can my former spouse substitute buying sprees with the child for child-support payments?

No. Purchases of gifts and clothing for a child do not relieve your former spouse from an obligation to pay you child support.

9.30   Are expenses such as child care supposed to be taken out of my child support?

No. Child-care expenses will be calculated as part of the Michigan Child Support Guidelines.

9.31   How does providing health insurance for my child affect my child-support amount?

If you pay the health insurance premium for your child, the amount you pay will be taken into account when calculating child support. You will receive a credit for the amount you pay per month for your child's health insurance premium.

9.32   Am I required to pay for my child's uninsured medical expenses from the child support I receive?

Yes, unless your decree provides otherwise, if you have sole physical custody of your child, then the first $357 per child, per year of uninsured health care costs are included in the child-support amount you receive. All uninsured health care costs in excess of $357 per child, per year are allocated between the parties as determined by the child-support guidelines.

9.33   Am I required to pay for the general, everyday expenses for my child with the child support I receive?

Yes, if you are receiving child support, under the guidelines, you are responsible for expenses for your child such as housing, clothing, school lunches, and the cost for activities.

However, if you have a 50/50 parenting time schedule, or close to it, you will provide for your child's day-to-day expenses when the child is with you, and the other parent will pay for those expenses when the child is in their care. You will need to coordinate with the other parent for purchases of major expenses.

9.34   Can my spouse be required by the decree to pay for our child's private elementary and high school education?

Probably not. The Michigan Child Support Guidelines make no specific provision for private education tuition. However, some parents agree to include a provision in the decree for payment of such tuition because both of them believe it is important for their child.

If you want your spouse to share this expense for your child, talk it over with your lawyer. Be sure to provide your attorney with information regarding tuition, fees, and other expenses related to private education.

9.35 Can my spouse be required by the decree to contribute financially to our child's college education?

The legal duty of a parent to support a child typically stops when the child reaches the age of majority and, therefore, does not include payment for college education. However, if your spouse agrees to pay this expense, it can be included in the final decree and it will be an enforceable court order. Such a provision is ordinarily included in a divorce decree only as a result of a negotiated settlement.

If your decree includes a provision for payment of college education expenses, be sure it is specific. Terms to consider include:

- What expenses are included? For example, tuition, room and board, books, fees, travel.
- Is there a limit? For example, up to the level of the cost of attendance at a specific institution or a certain dollar amount.
- When is the payment due?
- For what period of time does it continue?
- Are there any limits on the type of education that will be paid for?

The greater the detail in such a provision, the lower the risk is for misunderstanding or conflict years later.

10

Alimony

The mere mention of the word *alimony* might stir your emotions and start your stomach churning. If your spouse has filed for divorce and is seeking alimony, you might see it as a double injustice—your marriage is ending and you feel like you have to pay for it, too. If you are seeking *alimony,* also referred to as *spousal support,* you might feel hurt and confused that your spouse is resistant to helping support you, even though you may have interrupted your career to stay home and care for your children.

Learning more about Michigan's laws on alimony can help you move from your emotional reaction to the reality of possible outcomes in your case. Uncertainty about the precise amount of alimony that may be awarded or the number of years it might be paid is not unusual. Work closely with your lawyer. Be open to possibilities. Try looking at it from your spouse's perspective.

With the help of your lawyer, you will decide the best course of action to take toward an alimony decision you can live with after your divorce is over.

10.1   Which gets calculated first, child support or alimony?

Child support. Spousal support is determined from the income that is available after the amount of child support is determined.

10.2   What's the difference between *spousal support* and *alimony*?

In Michigan, alimony and spousal support have the same meaning.

10.3   How will I know if I am eligible to receive alimony?

Talk with your attorney about whether you are a candidate for alimony.

The opinions of Michigan judges about awarding alimony vary greatly. The court will consider the following factors when determining whether to award alimony to a party:

- Parties' past relations and conduct
- The length of your marriage
- Parties' ability to work
- Source and amount of property awarded to the parties
- Parties' ages
- Ability to pay spousal support
- Parties' present situation
- Parties' needs
- Parties' health
- Prior standard of living and whether the parties support others
- General principles of equity
- Your contributions to the marriage, including interruption of your career for the care of children or to support your spouse's career
- Your education, work history, health, income, and earning capacity
- Your overall financial situation compared to that of your spouse
- Your need for support
- Your spouse's ability to pay support

Every case for alimony is unique. Providing your lawyer with clear and detailed information about the facts of your marriage and current situation will allow him or her to make an alimony assessment in your case.

10.4 What information should I provide to my attorney if I want alimony?

If your attorney advises you that you may be a candidate for alimony, be sure to provide complete facts about your situation, including:

- A history of the interruptions in your education or career for the benefit of your spouse, including transfers or moves due to your spouse's employment
- A history of the interruptions in your education or career for raising children, including periods during which you worked part-time
- Your spouse's and your complete educational background, including the dates of schooling or training and degrees earned
- Your spouse's and your work history, including the names of employers, the dates of employment, duties, pay, and the reasons for leaving
- Any pensions or other benefits lost due to the interruption of your career for the benefit of the marriage
- Your health history, including any current diagnoses, treatments, limitations, and medications
- Your monthly living expenses, including anticipated future expenses such as health insurance and tax on alimony
- A complete list of the debts for you and your spouse
- Income for you and your spouse, including all sources

Also include any other facts that might support your need for alimony, such as other contributions you made to the marriage, upcoming medical treatment, or a lack of jobs in the field in which you were formerly employed.

No two alimony cases are alike. The better the information your lawyer has about your situation, the easier it will be for him or her to assess your case for alimony.

10.5   My spouse told me that because I had an affair during the marriage, I have no chance to get alimony even though I quit my job and have cared for our children for many years. Is it true that I have no case?

Your right to alimony will be based upon many factors, and "fault" for the end or breakdown of the marriage can be one factor considered, but the court must not assign disproportionate weight to that issue and having an affair is not an absolute or automatic bar to getting spousal support. However, if your affair had a financial impact on the marital estate, it may be taken into consideration when determining an award of alimony.

10.6   How is the amount of alimony calculated?

Unlike child support, there are not specific guidelines for determining the amount of alimony. A judge will look at the expenses and incomes of you and your spouse, after giving consideration to the payment and receipt of child support.

Judges are given a lot of discretion to make their own decision on alimony without the benefit of specific guidelines. Consequently, the outcome of an alimony ruling by a judge can be one of the most unpredictable aspects of your divorce.

10.7   My spouse makes a lot more money than he reports on our tax return, but he hides it. How can I prove my spouse's real income to show he can afford to pay alimony?

Alert your attorney to your concerns. Your lawyer can then take a number of actions to determine your spouse's income with greater accuracy. They are likely to include:

- More thorough discovery
- An examination of check registers and bank deposits
- Inquiries about travel
- Depositions of third parties who have knowledge of income or spending by your spouse
- Subpoena of records of places where your spouse has made large purchases or received income
- Comparison of income claimed with expenses paid
- Inquiries of purchases made in cash

Alimony

By partnering with your lawyer, you may be able to build a case to establish your spouse's actual income as greater than is shown on tax returns. If you filed joint tax returns, discuss with your lawyer any other implications of erroneous information on those returns.

10.8 I want to be sure the records on the alimony I pay are accurate, especially for tax purposes. What's the best way to ensure this?

If you are paying child support in addition to spousal support, your alimony payments should be made through the Michigan State Disbursement Unit (MiSDU) in Lansing. Alimony can be automatically withheld from your pay, just like your child support, or you can send the payment in to MiSDU yourself

By avoiding direct payments to your former spouse, you and he or she will have accurate records. To avoid an audit by the Internal Revenue Service, you must deduct the same amount of alimony that your spouse is reporting as income on your tax returns.

10.9 What effect does alimony have on my taxes?

If you are required to pay alimony pursuant to a court order, your alimony payments are tax deductible. Likewise, if you receive alimony pursuant to a court order, you must pay income tax on the amount received. For more information, please *see* questions 14.4 and 14.5 in chapter 14.

10.10 What types of payments are considered alimony?

Payments to a third party on behalf of your spouse under the terms of your divorce decree may be treated as alimony. These may include payments for your spouse's medical expenses, housing costs, taxes, and tuition. These payments are treated as if they were received by your spouse then paid to the third party. Additionally, if you pay the premiums on a life insurance policy that is owned by your spouse, those payments are considered alimony. Finally, if you are ordered to pay for expenses for a house owned by you and your spouse, some of your payments may be considered alimony.

10.11 How is the purpose of alimony different from the payment of my property settlement?

Spousal support and the division of property serve two distinct purposes, even though many of the factors for determining them are the same. The purpose of alimony is to provide support. In contrast, the purpose of a property division is to distribute the marital assets fairly between you and your spouse.

10.12 My spouse makes a lot more money than I do. Will I be awarded alimony to make up the difference in our income?

Although the purpose of alimony is to provide support, alimony awards are not used to equalize the incomes of the parties. Instead, alimony may be awarded to assist the economically disadvantaged spouse for the transitional period during and after the divorce, until he or she becomes economically self-sufficient. However, a disparity in income may be one factor the judge contemplates when considering an award of alimony.

10.13 How long can I expect to receive alimony?

Like your right to receive alimony, how long you will receive alimony will depend upon the facts of your case and the judge's philosophy toward alimony. In general, the longer your marriage, the stronger your case is for a long-term alimony award.

You may receive only temporary alimony, you may receive alimony for several years, or, in some cases, you could receive permanent alimony. Talk to your attorney about the facts of your case to get a clearer picture of the possible outcomes in your situation.

Unless you and your spouse agree otherwise, your alimony will terminate upon your remarriage or the death of either of you.

10.14 Does remarriage affect my alimony?

Yes. Under Michigan law, unless your divorce decree provides otherwise, alimony ends upon the remarriage of the recipient.

10.15 Does the death of my former spouse affect my alimony?

Yes. Under Michigan law, unless your decree provides otherwise, alimony ends upon the death of either party. There are ways to secure the payment of alimony to you with life insurance so that, upon your spouse's death, you receive a lump-sum payment of the total outstanding spousal support.

10.16 Do I have to keep paying alimony if my former spouse is now living with a new significant other?

Yes. Do not stop making your alimony payments. Instead, contact your attorney to seek a modification of the alimony award. Support may be reduced or terminated with a new court order if your former spouse is living with a new significant other.

10.17 Can I continue to collect alimony if I move to a different state?

Yes. The duty of your former spouse to follow a court order to pay alimony does not end simply because you move to another state, unless this is a specific provision in your decree.

10.18 What can I do if my spouse stops paying alimony?

If your spouse stops paying alimony, see your attorney about your options for enforcing your court order. The judge may order the support be taken from a source of your spouse's income or from a financial account belonging to your spouse.

If your spouse is intentionally refusing to pay spousal support, talk to your attorney about whether pursuing a contempt of court action would be effective. In a contempt action, your spouse may be ordered to appear in court and provide evidence explaining why support has not been paid. Possible consequences for contempt of court include a jail sentence or a fine.

10.19 Can I return to court to modify alimony?

It depends. If your divorce decree provides that your alimony order is "nonmodifiable," then it may not be modified. Also, your decree may not be modified to award alimony if alimony was not awarded in the original decree dissolving the marriage.

If there has been a material change in the circumstances of either you or your spouse, you may seek to have alimony modified. Examples include a serious illness or the loss or obtaining of a job.

A request to modify alimony for the purposes of seeking additional alimony may not be filed if the time for payment of alimony allowed under your original decree has already passed.

If you think you have a basis to modify your alimony, contact your attorney at once to be sure a timely modification request is filed with the court.

11

Division of Property

You never imagined that you would face losing the house you and your spouse so happily moved into—the house where you celebrated family traditions and spent countless hours making it "home." Your spouse wants it and your lawyer says it might have to be sold.

During a divorce, you will have to decide whether you or your spouse will take ownership of everything from bathroom towels to the stock portfolio. Suddenly, you find yourself having a strong attachment to that lamp in the family room or the painting in the hallway. Why does the collection of coins suddenly take on new meaning?

Do your best to reach agreement regarding dividing household goods. Enlist the support of your attorney in deciding which assets should be valued by an expert, such as the family business or real estate. From tax consequences to replacement value, there are many factors to consider in deciding whether to fight to keep an asset, to give it to your spouse, or to have it sold.

Like all aspects of your divorce, take one step at a time. By starting with the items most easily divided, you and your spouse can avoid paying lawyers to litigate the value of that 1980s album collection.

11.1 What system does Michigan use for dividing property?

Michigan law provides for an equitable or fair, but not necessarily equal, division of the property and debts acquired during your marriage.

129

Regardless of how title is held, the court can use its discretion to make a division of the marital assets and marital debts. That will require an assessment of what assets and debt are *marital* (acquired during the marriage).

In many cases this may mean an equal division, but as little as one-third of the assets awarded to one party and two-thirds to the other may still be considered *equitable*. The court will consider a number of factors, including your debts, the economic circumstances of you and your spouse, and the history of contributions to the marriage.

11.2   What does *community property* mean?

Community property is a term used in several states that have a community property system for dividing assets in a divorce. In states having community property laws, each spouse holds a one-half interest in most property acquired during the marriage. Because Michigan is not a community property state, community property laws do not apply.

11.3   How is it determined who gets the house?

The first issue to be decided regarding the family home is the determination of who will retain possession of it while the divorce is pending. Later, it must be decided whether the house will be sold or whether it will be awarded to you or your spouse.

Several factors to consider when determining the disposition of the home are:

- Who can afford the mortgage and expenses associated with the home
- Who has custody of the children
- Whether the house is premarital
- Whether there are other assets in the marital estate to offset the value of the home

Talk with your lawyer about your options and to consider the above factors. If you and your spouse are unable to reach agreement regarding the house, the judge will decide who keeps it or whether it will be sold.

11.4 Should I sell the house during the divorce proceedings?

Selling your home is a big decision. To help you decide what is right for you, ask yourself these questions:

- What will be the impact on my children if the home is sold?
- Can I afford to stay in the house after the divorce?
- After the divorce, will I be willing to give the house and yard the time, money, and physical energy required for its maintenance?
- Is it necessary for me to sell the house to pay a share of the equity to my spouse, or are there other options?
- Would my life be easier if I were in a smaller or simpler home?
- Would I prefer to move closer to the support of friends and family?
- What is the state of the housing market in my community?
- What are the benefits of remaining in this house?
- Can I retain the existing mortgage or will I have to refinance?
- Will I have a higher or lower interest rate if I sell the house and buy a new one?
- Can I see myself living in a different home?
- Will I have the means to acquire another home?
- If I don't retain the home and my spouse asks for it, what effect will this have on my custody case?
- Will my spouse agree to the sale of the house?
- What will be the real estate commission?
- What will be the costs of preparing the house for sale?

Selling a home is more than just a legal or financial decision. Consider what is important to you in creating your life after divorce when deciding whether to sell your home.

11.5 How is it determined how much our house is worth?

In a divorce, the value of your home can be determined a number of ways. You and your spouse can agree to the value of your home. You can seek advice from a local real estate agent on the approximate value of your home through a market analysis. Or, for a more authoritative valuation, you can hire a professional real estate appraiser to determine the value of your home. Talk to your attorney to determine the best method to value your home in your divorce.

11.6 My house is worth less than what is owed. What are my options?

Talk with your lawyer and consider consulting with a mortgage specialist. It is important to get an accurate assessment of the value of your house. Consider working with a professional, such as an appraiser or realtor, to obtain the estimated fair market value of your home. If your house is *underwater,* meaning you owe more on the mortgage than your house is worth, you may decide to list your house for sale and keep it on the market while continuing to make your mortgage payments. Another option to consider is a *short sale,* where the lender accepts less money for your house than you owe. Seek advice from your lawyer and other financial experts to determine which option is best for you.

11.7 What is meant by *equity* in my home?

Regardless of who is awarded your house, the court will consider whether the spouse not receiving the house should be compensated for the equity in the house. *Equity* is the difference between the value of the home and the amount of debt, such as a mortgage or home equity line of credit, owed against the property.

For example, if the first mortgage is $50,000 and the second mortgage from a home equity loan is $10,000, the total debt owed against the house is $60,000. If your home is valued at $100,000, the equity in your home is $40,000. (The $100,000 value less the $60,000 in mortgages equals $40,000 in equity.) You and your spouse would each be entitled to $20,000 of the equity in the marital home if property is divided equally.

If one of the parties remains in the home, the issue of how to give the other party his or her share of the equity must be considered.

Division of Property

11.8 How will the equity in our house be divided?

If your home is going to be sold, the equity in the home will most likely be divided at the time of the sale, after the costs of the sale have been paid.

If either you or your spouse will be awarded the house, there are a number of options for the other party being compensated for his or her share of the equity in the marital home. These could include:

- The spouse who does not receive the house receives other assets (for example, retirement funds) to compensate for his or her respective share of the equity.
- The person who remains in the home agrees to refinance the home at some future date and to pay the other party his or her share of the equity.
- The parties agree that the property be sold at a future date, or upon the happening of a certain event such as the youngest child completing high school or the remarriage of the party keeping the home.

Because the residence is often among the most valuable assets considered in a divorce, it is important that you and your attorney discuss the details of its disposition. These include:

- Valuation of the property
- Refinancing to remove a party from liability for the mortgage
- The dates on which certain actions should be taken, such as listing the home for sale
- The real estate agent
- Costs for preparing the home for sale
- Making mortgage payments

If you and your spouse do not agree regarding which of you will remain in the home, the court will decide who keeps it or may order the property sold.

11.9 If my spouse signs a *quitclaim deed,* does that remove his obligation to repay the mortgage?

No. *A quitclaim deed* is a legal document that transfers one person's interest in real property to another person. However, removing his name from the title of your property will not remove his obligation to repay the mortgage. You and your spouse signed a contract with the lender to repay the debt you borrowed to purchase your home. Thus, removing your spouse's name from the title on the property does not remove his obligation to repay the mortgage. To remove your spouse from the obligation, you must seek a refinance of your current mortgage. A refinance involves obtaining a new mortgage loan to pay off the existing mortgage.

11.10 Who keeps all the household goods until the decree is signed?

The court will ordinarily not make any decisions about who keeps the household goods on a temporary basis. Most couples attempt to resolve these issues on their own rather than incur legal fees to dispute household goods on a temporary basis. However, the court may enter an order restraining the parties from transferring, selling, or destroying household goods during the divorce process so that the goods remain intact and can be divided by the decree.

11.11 How can I reduce the risk that assets will be hidden, transferred, or destroyed by my spouse?

Consulting with an attorney before the filing of divorce can reduce the risk that assets will be hidden, transferred, or destroyed by your spouse. This is especially important if your spouse has a history of destroying property, incurring substantial debt, or transferring money without your knowledge.

These are among the possible actions you and your attorney can consider together:

- Placing your family heirlooms or other valuables in a safe location
- Transferring some portion of financial accounts prior to filing for divorce
- Preparing an inventory of the personal property
- Taking photographs or video of the property
- Obtaining copies of important records or statements
- Obtaining a restraining order before your spouse is served with notice of the divorce

Plans to leave the marital home should also be discussed in detail with your attorney so that any actions taken early in your case are consistent with your ultimate goals.

Speak candidly with your lawyer about your concerns so that a plan can be developed that provides a level of protection that is appropriate to your circumstances.

11.12 How are assets such as cars, boats, and furniture divided, and when does this happen?

In most cases spouses are able to reach their own agreements about how to divide personal property, such as household furnishings and vehicles.

If you and your spouse disagree about how to divide certain items, it can be wise to consider which are truly valuable to you, financially or otherwise. Perhaps some of them can be easily replaced. Always look to see whether it is a good use of your attorney fees to argue over items of personal property. If a negotiated settlement cannot be reached, the issue of the division of your property will be made by the judge at trial.

11.13 How do I value our used personal property?

In a divorce, your personal property will be valued at its fair market value. The *fair market value* is the price a buyer would be willing to pay for the item at a garage sale or on an online auction website. For example, if you bought a sofa for $3,000 five years ago, the fair market value of the couch is what you could sell it for at a garage sale today. The fair market value is not how much the couch was when you bought it or how much it will cost to replace the couch. Instead, the value of your personal property is what you could reasonably sell it for in its current used condition.

11.14 My wife and I own a coin collection. How will our collection be valued and divided in our divorce?

If you own a unique collection, such as a gun, art, or coin collection, talk with your attorney about how to value the collection. It may be that you will need the collection appraised by an expert who has specialized training and knowledge to determine its value. If you and your spouse cannot agree on who will keep the collection, it is possible the judge will order the collection to be sold. The judge may also order you to divide the collection between you and your spouse.

11.15 What is meant by a *property inventory,* and how detailed should mine be?

A *property inventory* is a listing of the property you own. It may also include a brief description of the property. Discuss with your attorney the level of inventory detail needed to benefit your case.

Factors to consider when creating your inventory may include:

- The extent to which you anticipate you and your spouse will disagree regarding the division of your property
- Whether you anticipate a dispute regarding the value of the property either you or your spouse is retaining
- Whether you will have continued access to the property if a later inventory is needed or whether your spouse will retain control of the property
- Whether you or your spouse are likely to disagree about which items are premarital, inherited, or gifts from someone other than your spouse

In addition to creating an inventory, your attorney may request that you prepare a list of the property that you and your spouse have already divided or a list of the items you want but your spouse has not agreed to give to you.

If you do not have continued access to your property, talk to your attorney about taking photographs or obtaining access to the property to complete your inventory.

11.16 What happens to our individual checking and savings accounts during and after the divorce?

Regardless of whose name is on the account, bank accounts may be considered marital assets and may be divided by the court. Discuss with your attorney the benefits of a temporary restraining order to protect bank accounts, how to retain access or obtain an accounting of these accounts, how to use these accounts while the case is pending, and the date on which financial accounts should be valued.

11.17 How and when are liquid assets like bank accounts and stocks divided?

Talk with your attorney early in your case about the benefits of a temporary restraining order to reduce the risk that your spouse will transfer money out of financial accounts or transfer other assets.

In some cases couples will agree to divide bank accounts equally at the outset of the case. In other cases, the parties will agree to maintain the *status quo,* meaning the parties will continue to pay bills and expenses from the marital accounts, as they always have, during the pendency of the divorce action. For example, if your wife has always deposited her paycheck into the joint account from which you have paid all the bills and expenses, that practice would continue during the divorce proceedings. Often, the court will enter an order requiring the parties to maintain the *status quo,* in which case there would be legal consequences if one party violated the *status quo* procedures.

Discuss with your attorney whether you should keep an accounting of how you spend money used from a bank account while your divorce is in progress.

Stocks are ordinarily a part of the final agreement for the division of property and debts. If you and your spouse cannot agree on how your investments should be divided, the judge will make the decision at trial.

11.18 How is pet custody determined?

Pet custody is determined on a case-by-case basis. Michigan law is not well established on the matter of pet custody. Factors that courts have considered include:

- Who held title to the pet?
- Who provided care for the pet?
- Who will best be able to meet the pet's needs?

Some courts have awarded the pet to one party and given the other party certain rights, such as:

- Specific periods of time to spend with the pet
- The right to care for the pet when the other person is not able to
- The right to be informed of the pet's health condition

If it is important to you to be awarded one of your family pets, discuss the matter with your attorney. It may be possible to reach a pet care agreement with your spouse that will allow you to share possession of and responsibility for your pets.

11.19 How will our property in another state be divided?

For the purposes of dividing your assets, out-of-state property is treated the same as property in Michigan. Although a Michigan court cannot order a change in the title to property located in another state, a judge can order your spouse either to turn the property over to you or to sign a deed or other document to transfer title to you.

11.20 Are all of the assets—such as property, bank accounts, and inheritances—that I had prior to my marriage still going to be mine after the divorce?

It depends. In many cases the court will allow a party to retain an asset brought into the marriage (a *premarital asset*), but the following are questions the court will consider in making its determination:

- Can the premarital asset be clearly traced? For example, if you continue to own a vehicle that you brought into the marriage, it is likely that it will be awarded to you as your separate property. However, if you brought a vehicle into the marriage, sold it during the marriage, and spent the proceeds, it is less likely that the court will consider awarding you its value.

- Did you keep the property separate and titled in your name, or did you commingle it with marital assets? Premarital assets you kept separate may be more likely to be awarded to you.

- Did the other spouse contribute to the increase in the value of the premarital asset, and can the value of that increase be proven? For example, suppose a woman owned a home prior to her marriage. After the marriage, the parties live in the home, continuing to make mortgage payments and improvements to the home. At the time of the divorce, the husband seeks a portion of the equity in the home. The court might consider the value of the home at the time of the

138

marriage, any contributions to the increase in equity made by the husband, and the evidence of the value of those contributions.

11.21 Will I get to keep my engagement ring?

If your engagement ring was given to you prior to your marriage, it will be considered a gift and treated as premarital property that you can keep.

11.22 What does it mean to *commingle* property?

Commingling occurs when one spouse's separate property is mixed or combined with the marital property, such that the separate property can no longer be distinguished from the marital property.

11.23 Can I keep gifts and inheritances I received during the marriage?

Similar rules apply to gifts and inheritances received during the marriage as apply to premarital assets, that is, assets you owned prior to the marriage.

Gifts that you and your spouse gave to each other may be treated as any other marital asset. For gifts received during the marriage from a third party, such as a gift from a parent, the court will need to determine whether the gift was made to one party or to both. Whether you will be entitled to keep assets you inherited, assuming they are still in existence, will depend upon the unique circumstances of your case. When dividing the marital estate, the court may consider the fact that one spouse is allowed to keep substantial nonmarital assets such as an inheritance.

The following factors increase the probability that you will be entitled to keep your inheritance:

- It has been kept separate from the marital assets, such as a separate account.
- It is titled in your name only.
- It can be clearly identified.
- It has not been commingled with marital assets.
- Your spouse has not contributed to its care, operation, or improvement.

It is less likely that you will be awarded your full inheritance if:

- It was commingled with marital assets.
- Its origin cannot be traced.
- You have placed your spouse's name on the title.
- Your spouse has contributed to the increase in the value of the inheritance.

If keeping your inheritance is important to you, talk to your attorney about the information needed to build your case.

11.24   If my spouse and I can't decide who gets what, who decides? Can that person's decision be contested?

If you and your spouse cannot agree on the division of your property, the judge will make the determination after considering the evidence at your trial.

If either party is dissatisfied with the decision reached by the judge, an appeal to a higher court is possible, although often a costly and lengthy process.

11.25   How are the values of property determined?

The value of some assets, like bank accounts, is usually not disputed. The value of other assets, such as homes or personal property, is more likely to be disputed.

If your case proceeds to trial, you may give your opinion of the value of property you own. You or your spouse may also have certain property appraised by an expert. In such cases it may be necessary to have the appraiser appear at trial to give testimony regarding the appraisal and the value of the asset.

If you own substantial assets for which the value is likely to be disputed, talk to your attorney early in your case about the benefits and costs of expert witnesses.

11.26   What does *date of valuation* mean?

Because the value of assets can go up or down while a divorce is pending, it can be necessary to determine a set date for valuing the marital assets. This is referred to as the *date of valuation*. You and your spouse can agree on the date the

Division of Property

assets should be valued. If you cannot agree, the judge will decide the date of valuation.

Among the most common dates used are the date of separation, the date of the filing of the divorce complaint, or the date of the divorce trial.

11.27 Who gets the interest from certificates of deposit and dividends from stock holdings during the divorce proceedings?

Whether you or your spouse receives interest from these assets is decided as a part of the overall division of your property and debts.

11.28 Does each one of our financial accounts have to be divided in half if we agree to an equal division of our assets?

No. Rather than incurring the administrative challenges and the expense of dividing each asset in half, you and your spouse can decide that one of you will take certain assets equal to the value of assets taken by the spouse. If necessary, one of you can agree to make a cash payment to the other to make an equitable division.

11.29 Is my *health savings account* an asset that can be divided in the divorce?

Yes. A *health savings account (HSA)* is a tax-advantaged medical savings account to which contributions may be made by employees, employers, or both. Your HSA is an asset to be included in the property distribution and may be divided pursuant to your divorce decree and transferred to another HSA. A division pursuant to a decree does not constitute a distribution and is thus a tax-free transfer. Some HSA accounts cannot be divided and must remain intact for the benefit of the employee only. In that case, the spouse would receive other retirement assets or a lump-sum cash payment to equalize the division of the marital estate.

11.30 I worked very hard for years to support my family while my spouse completed an advanced degree. Do I have a right to any of my spouse's future earnings?

Your contributions during the marriage are a factor to be considered in both the division of the property and debts, as well as any award of alimony. Be sure to give your attorney a complete history of your contributions to the marriage and ask about their impact on the outcome of your case.

11.31 What factors determine whether I can get a share of my spouse's business?

Many factors determine whether you will get a share of your spouse's business and in what form you might receive it. Among the factors the court will look at are:

- Whether your spouse owned the business prior to your marriage
- Your role, if any, in operating the business or increasing its value
- The overall division of the property and debts

If you or your spouse owns a business, it is important that you work with your attorney early in your case to develop a strategy for valuing the business and making your case for how it should be treated in the division of property and debts.

11.32 My spouse and I have owned and run our own business together for many years. Can I be forced out of it?

Deciding what should happen with a family business when divorce occurs can be a challenge. Because of the risk for future conflict between you and your spouse, the value of the business is likely to be substantially decreased if you both remain owners.

In discussing your options with your lawyer, consider the following questions:

- If one spouse retains ownership of the business, are there enough other assets for the other spouse to receive a fair share of the total marital assets?
- Which spouse has the skills and experience to continue running the business?

- What would you do if you weren't working in the business?
- What is the value of the business?
- What is the market for the business if it were to be sold?
- Could you remain an employee of the business for some period of time even if you were not an owner?

You and your spouse know your business best. With the help of your lawyers, you may be able to create a settlement that can satisfy you both. If not, the judge will make the decision for you at trial.

11.33 I suspect my spouse is hiding assets, but I can't prove it. How can I protect myself if I discover later that I was right?

Ask your lawyer to include language in your divorce decree to address your concern. Insist that it include an acknowledgment by your spouse that the agreement was based upon a full and complete disclosure of your spouse's financial condition. Discuss with your lawyer a provision that allows for setting aside the agreement if it is later discovered that assets were hidden.

11.34 My spouse says I'm not entitled to a share of his stock options because he gets to keep them only if he stays employed with his company. What are my rights?

Stock options are often a very valuable asset. They are also one of the most complex issues when dividing assets during a divorce for these, among other, reasons:

- Each company has its own rules about awarding and exercising stock options.
- Complete information is needed from the employer.
- There are different methods for calculating the value of stock options.
- The reasons the options were given can impact the valuation and division. For example, some are given for future performance and may be considered separate property.

- There are cost and tax considerations when options are exercised.

Rather than being awarded a portion of the stock options themselves, you are likely to receive a share of the proceeds when the stock options are exercised.

If either you or your spouse owns stock options, begin discussing this asset with your attorney early in your case to allow sufficient time to settle the issues or to be well prepared for trial.

11.35 What is a *prenuptial agreement,* and how might it affect the property settlement phase of the divorce?

A *prenuptial agreement,* sometimes referred to as a *pre-marital* or *antenuptial agreement,* is a contract entered into between two people prior to their marriage. It can include provisions for how assets and debts will be divided in the event the marriage is terminated, as well as provisions regarding alimony.

Your property settlement is likely to be impacted by the terms of your prenuptial agreement if the agreement is upheld as valid by the court.

11.36 Can a prenuptial agreement be contested during the divorce?

Yes. The court may consider many factors in determining whether to uphold your prenuptial agreement, but the court has imposed the following requirements for an enforceable prenuptial agreement:

- It must be in writing and signed by both parties.
- It must have been entered into voluntarily, without fraud, mistake, or duress and with full disclosure of both parties' assets and debts.
- It must be fair and not unconscionable when executed, and the circumstances must not have changed so much that by the time the agreement is enforceable, enforcement would be unconscionable.

If you have a prenuptial agreement, bring a copy of it to the initial consultation with your attorney. Be sure to provide your lawyer with a detailed history of the facts and circumstances surrounding reaching and signing the agreement, including whether you were represented by an attorney at the time you negotiated the agreement and how much time you had to review and revise the agreement before your marriage took place.

11.37 I'm Jewish and want my husband to cooperate with obtaining a *get*, which is a divorce document under our religion. Can I get a court order for this?

Talk to your lawyer about obtaining a *get* cooperation clause in your divorce decree, including a provision regarding who should pay for it. Only the husband may obtain the *get*.

11.38 Who will get the frozen embryo of my egg and my spouse's sperm that we have stored at the health clinic?

The law on this issue is not yet established in Michigan. The terms of your contract with the clinic may impact the rights you and your spouse have to the embryo, so provide a copy of it to your attorney for review. If permissible under your contract, you and your spouse may want to consider donating the embryo to another couple.

11.39 Will debts be considered when determining the division of the property?

Yes. The court will consider any debts incurred during the course of the marriage when dividing the property. For example, if you are awarded a car valued at $12,000, but you owe a $10,000 debt on the same vehicle, the court will take that debt into consideration in the overall division of the assets. Similarly, if one spouse agrees to pay substantial marital credit card debt, this obligation may also be considered in the final determination of the division of property and debts.

If your spouse incurred debts that you believe should be his or her sole responsibility, tell your attorney. Some debts may be considered nonmarital and treated separately from other debts incurred during the marriage. For example, if your spouse spent large sums of money on gambling or illegal drugs without your knowledge, you may be able to argue that those debts should be the sole responsibility of your spouse.

11.40 What is a *property settlement agreement*?

A *property settlement agreement* is a written document that includes all of the financial agreements you and your spouse have reached in your divorce. This may include the division of property, debts, child support, alimony, insurance, and attorney fees.

The property settlement may be a separate document, or it may be incorporated into the *decree of dissolution,* which is the final court order dissolving your marriage.

11.41 What happens after my spouse and I approve the property settlement agreement? Do we still have to go to court?

Not necessarily. After you and your spouse approve and sign the property settlement agreement or decree, it must still be approved by your judge. If you choose, the judge can approve your decree at a final hearing. A final hearing can be scheduled after the passing of the sixty-day mandatory waiting period under Michigan law if you do not have minor children. If there are minor children, the court imposes a six-month waiting period, but the court may agree to waive that waiting period if you and your spouse have resolved the property settlement and all matters pertaining to your minor children.

If a property settlement agreement is reached by the parties, a court date for your final hearing can often be obtained earlier than a trial date because a final hearing requires much less time than a trial.

11.42 If my spouse and I think our property settlement agreement is fair, why does the judge have to approve it?

The judge has a duty to ensure that all property settlement agreements in divorces are fair, reasonable, and equitable under Michigan law. For this reason, your judge must review your agreement. The judge can consider the facts and circumstances of your case when reviewing the agreement. Not every case will result in an equal division of the assets and debts from the marriage, although this is very common.

11.43 What happens to the property distribution if one of us dies before the divorce proceedings are completed?

If your spouse dies prior to your divorce decree being entered, you will be considered married and treated as a surviving spouse under the law.

11.44 After our divorce is final, can the property agreement be modified?

Generally, provisions in your property settlement agreement or decree dealing with the distribution of your assets and debts are not modifiable. Absent an uncommon instance of fraud, duress, or newly discovered evidence, the property settlement agreement cannot be modified.

12

Benefits: Insurance, Retirement, and Pensions

During your marriage, you might have taken certain employment benefits for granted. You might not have given much thought each month to having insurance through your spouse's work. When you find yourself in a divorce, suddenly these benefits come to the forefront of your mind.

You might also, even unconsciously, have seen your own employment retirement benefits as belonging to you and not to your spouse and referred to "my 401(k)" or "my pension." After all, you are the one who went to work every day to earn it, right?

When you divorce, some benefits arising from your spouse's employment will end, some may continue for a period of time, and others may be divided between you. Retirement funds, in particular, are often one of the valuable marital assets to be divided in a divorce.

Whether the benefits are from your employer or from your spouse's employer, with your attorney's help you will develop a better understanding of which benefits the law considers to be "yours," "mine," and "ours" for continuing or dividing.

12.1 Will my children continue to have health coverage through my spouse's work even though we're divorcing?

If either you or your spouse currently provides health insurance for your children, it is very likely that the court will order the insurance to remain in place until your child reaches the age of majority, or for as long as it remains available and support is being paid for your child.

The cost of insurance for the children will be taken into consideration in determining the amount of child support to be paid.

12.2 Will I continue to have health insurance through my spouse's work after the divorce?

It depends. If your spouse currently provides health insurance for you, you may be treated as a spouse for health insurance purposes for six months following the entry of your divorce decree. However, most insurance companies refuse to treat a person as a spouse after the entry of the divorce decree.

Investigate the cost of continuing on your spouse's employer-provided plans under a federal law known as *COBRA (Consolidated Omnibus Budget Reconciliation Act)* after the expiration of your previous coverage. This coverage can be maintained for up to three years. However, the cost can be very high, so you will want to determine whether it's a realistic option.

If you have no other health insurance and it is permitted by your spouse's insurance company, talk to your attorney about including a provision in your decree keeping you on your spouse's health insurance policy for the six-month period.

Begin early to investigate your eligibility for coverage on your spouse's health insurance plan after the entry of the decree and your options for your future health insurance. The cost of your health care is an important factor when pursuing spousal support and planning your postdivorce budget.

12.3 What is a *qualified domestic relations order*?

A *qualified domestic relations order (QDRO)* is a court order that requires a retirement or pension plan administrator to pay you the share of your former spouse's retirement that was awarded to you in the decree.

Obtaining a QDRO is a critical step in the divorce process. It can be a complex document, and a number of steps are required to reduce future concerns about enforcement and to fully protect your rights. These court orders must comply with numerous technical rules and be approved by the plan administrator, which is often located outside Michigan.

Whenever possible, court orders dividing retirement plans should be entered at the same time as the divorce decree.

12.4   How many years must I have been married before I'm eligible to receive a part of my spouse's retirement fund or pension?

To be eligible to receive a part of your spouse's retirement or pension fund, some companies require that you be married for a certain length of time. However, even if your marriage is not of long duration, you may be entitled to a portion of your spouse's retirement fund or pension accumulated during the marriage. For example, if you were married for three years and your spouse contributed $10,000 to a 401(k) plan during the marriage, it is possible that the court would award you half of the value of the contribution when dividing your property and debts.

12.5   I contributed to my pension plan for ten years before I got married. Will my spouse get half of my entire pension?

Probably not. It is more likely the court will award your spouse only a portion of your retirement that was acquired during the marriage.

If either you or your spouse made premarital contributions to a pension or retirement plan, be sure to let your attorney know. This is information essential to determine which portion of the retirement plan should be treated as "premarital" and thus unlikely to be shared.

12.6   I plan to keep my same job after my divorce. Will my former spouse get half of the money I contribute to my retirement plan after my divorce?

No. Your former spouse should be entitled to a portion of your retirement accumulated only during the marriage.

Talk with your attorney so that the language of the court order ensures protection of your postdivorce retirement contributions.

12.7 Am I still entitled to a share of my spouse's retirement even though I never contributed to one during our twenty-five-year marriage?

Probably. Retirements are often the most valuable asset accumulated during a marriage. Consequently, your judge will consider the retirement along with all of the other marital assets and debts when determining a fair division.

12.8 My lawyer says I'm entitled to a share of my spouse's retirement. How can I find out how much I get and when I'm eligible to receive it?

More than one factor will determine your rights to collect from your spouse's retirement. One factor will be the terms of the court order dividing the retirement. The court order will tell you whether you are entitled to a set dollar amount, a percentage, or a fraction to be determined based upon the length of your marriage and how long your spouse continues working. For a defined benefit plan, such as a pension, the fraction used by the court to determine how much you are eligible to receive will be the number of years you were married while your spouse was employed at that company divided by the total number of years your spouse is employed with the company.

Another factor will be the terms of the retirement plan itself. Some provide for lump-sum withdrawals; others issue payments in monthly installments. Review the terms of your court order and contact the plan administrator to obtain the clearest understanding of your rights and benefits.

12.9 If I am eligible to receive my spouse's retirement benefits, when am I eligible to begin collecting them? Do I have to be sixty-five to collect them?

It depends upon the terms of your spouse's retirement plan. In some cases it is possible to begin receiving your share at the earliest date your spouse is eligible to receive them, regardless of whether he or she elects to do so. Check the terms of your spouse's plan to learn your options.

151

12.10 What happens if my former spouse is old enough to receive benefits but I'm not?

Ordinarily, you will be eligible to begin receiving your share of the benefits when your former spouse begins receiving his or hers. Depending upon the plan, you may be eligible to receive them sooner. Check the terms of your spouse's plan to learn your options.

12.11 Am I entitled to *cost-of-living* increases on my share of my spouse's retirement?

It depends. If your spouse has a retirement plan that includes a provision for a *cost-of-living allowance (COLA),* talk to your lawyer about whether this can be included in the court order dividing the retirement.

12.12 Does the death of my spouse affect the payout of retirement benefits to me or to our children?

It depends upon both the nature of your spouse's retirement plan and the terms of the court order dividing the retirement. If you want to be eligible for survivorship benefits from your spouse's pension, discuss this issue with your attorney before your case is settled or goes to trial. He or she can advise you.

Some plans allow only a surviving spouse or former spouse to be a beneficiary. Others may allow for the naming of an alternate beneficiary, such as your children.

12.13 Can I still collect on my former spouse's Social Security benefits if he or she passes on before I do?

It depends. You may be eligible to receive benefits if:

- You were married to your spouse for ten or more years.
- You are not remarried.
- You are at least sixty-two years old.
- The benefit you would receive based on your own earning record is less than the benefit you would receive from your former spouse.

For more information, contact your local Social Security Administration office or visit the SSA website at www.ssa.gov.

12.14 What orders might the court enter regarding life insurance?

The judge may order you or your spouse to maintain a life insurance policy to ensure that future support payments, such as child support and alimony, are made. In most cases you will be required to pay for your own life insurance after your divorce, and you should include this as an expense in your monthly budget.

12.15 Because we share children, should I consider my spouse as a beneficiary on my life insurance?

It depends upon your intentions. If your intention is to give the money to your former spouse, by all means name the other parent as beneficiary.

However, if you intend the life insurance proceeds to be used for the benefit of your children, talk with your attorney about your options. You may consider naming a trustee to manage the life insurance proceeds on behalf of your children, and there may be reasons to choose someone other than your former spouse.

12.16 Can the court require in the decree that I be the beneficiary of my spouse's insurance policy, as long as the children are minors or indefinitely?

When a court order is entered for life insurance, it is ordinarily for the purposes of ensuring payment of future support and will terminate when the support obligation has ended. Naming you as the beneficiary on your spouse's insurance policy for purposes of ensuring payment of future child support is one option. The court may also name the children directly as beneficiaries or require a trust be established to receive the life insurance proceeds on behalf of your children.

12.17 My spouse is in the military. What are my rights to benefits after the divorce?

As the former spouse of a military member, the types of benefits to which you may be entitled are typically determined by the number of years you were married, the number of years your spouse was in the military while you were married, and whether or not you have remarried. Be sure you obtain accurate information about these dates.

Among the benefits for which you may be eligible are:

- A portion of your spouse's military retirement pay
- A survivor benefit in the event of your spouse's death
- Health care or participation in a temporary, transitional health care program
- Ability to keep your military identification card
- Use of certain military facilities, such as the commissary

Educate yourself about your right to future military benefits so that you can plan for your future with clarity. If your divorce is still pending, contact your base legal office, or, for more information, visit www.dfas.mil/dfas/garnishment, and then click on the link *Former Spouses' Protection Act* or the website for the branch of the military of which your spouse was a member.

13

Division of Debts

Throughout a marriage, most couples will have disagreements about money from time to time. You might think extra money should be spent on a family vacation, but your spouse might insist it should be saved for your retirement. You might think it's time to finally buy a new car, but your spouse thinks you driving the ten-year-old van for two more years is a better idea.

If you and your spouse had different philosophies about saving and spending during your marriage, chances are you will have some differing opinions when dividing your debts in divorce. What you both can count on is that Michigan law provides that, to reach a fair outcome, the payment of debts must also be taken into consideration when dividing the assets from your marriage.

There are steps you can take to ensure the best outcome possible when it comes to dividing your marital debt. These include providing accurate and complete debt information to your lawyer and asking your lawyer to include provisions in your divorce decree to protect you in the future if your spouse refuses to pay his or her share.

Regardless of how the debts from your marriage are divided, know that you will gradually build your independent financial success when making a fresh start after your divorce is final.

13.1 Who is responsible for paying credit card bills and making house payments during the divorce proceedings?

In most cases, the court will not make decisions regarding the payment of credit card debt on a temporary basis. Work with your attorney and your spouse to reach a temporary agreement. Discuss the importance of making at least minimum payments on time to avoid substantial finance charges and late fees.

Typically, the courts will order the parties to maintain the financial *status quo,* meaning all marital income will continue to be utilized to support the bills and expenses of the parties, regardless of who remains in the marital home during the pendency of the divorce.

13.2 What, if anything, should I be doing with the credit card companies as we go through the divorce?

If possible, it is best to obtain some separate credit prior to the divorce. This will help you establish credit in your own name and help you with necessary purchases following a separation.

Begin by obtaining a copy of your credit report from at least two of the three nationwide consumer reporting companies: Experian, Equifax, or TransUnion. *The Fair Credit Reporting Act* entitles you to a free copy of your credit report from each of these three companies every twelve months. To order your free annual report online, go to www.annualcreditreport.com, call (877) 322-8228, or complete an Annual Credit Report Request Form and mail it to: Annual Credit Report Request Service, P.O. Box 105281, Atlanta, GA 30348-5281. You can print the form from the *Federal Trade Commission* website at www.ftc.gov/credit.

Your spouse may have incurred debt using your name. This information is important to relay to your attorney. If you and your spouse have joint credit card accounts, contact any credit card company to close the account. Do the same if your spouse is an authorized user on any of your accounts. You may not be allowed to close the accounts while the divorce is pending if a *status quo* order is in place, but you should be prepared to close the accounts immediately upon entry of the divorce decree.

If you want to maintain credit with a company, ask to have a new account in your own name. Be sure to let your spouse know if you close an account he or she has been using.

13.3   How is credit card debt divided?

Credit card debt will be divided as a part of the overall division of the marital property and debts. Just as in the division of property, the court considers what is equitable, or fair, in your case.

If your spouse has exclusively used a credit card for purposes that did not benefit the family, such as gambling, talk with your attorney. In most cases the court will not review a lengthy history of how you and your spouse used the credit cards, but there can be exceptions.

13.4   Am I responsible for repayment of my spouse's student loans?

It depends. If your spouse incurred student loans prior to the marriage, it is most likely that he or she will be ordered to pay that debt.

If the debt was incurred during the marriage, how the funds were used may have an impact on who is ordered to pay them. For example, if your spouse borrowed $3,000 during the marriage for tuition, it is likely your spouse will be ordered to pay that debt. However, if a $3,000 student loan was taken out by your spouse, but $1,000 of it was used for a family vacation, then the court would be more likely to order the debt shared.

The court may also consider payment on student loan debt when calculating the amount of child support to be paid.

If you were a joint borrower on your spouse's student loan and your spouse fails to pay the loan, the lender may attempt to collect from you even if your spouse has been ordered to pay the debt.

If either you or your spouse has student loan debt, be sure to give your attorney the complete history regarding the debt and ask about the most likely outcome under the facts of your case.

13.5 During the divorce proceedings, am I still responsible for debt my spouse continues to accrue?

It depends. In most cases the court will order each of the parties to be responsible for his or her own post-separation debts. In some cases, the date for dividing debt is when the parties separated households and, in others, it is the date the complaint for divorce was filed.

13.6 During the marriage my spouse applied for and received several credit cards without my knowledge. Am I responsible for them?

It depends. The court will consider the overall fairness of the property and debt division when deciding who should pay this debt. If your spouse bought items with the cards and intends to keep those items, it is likely that she or he will be ordered to pay the debt incurred for the purchases.

The credit card companies are unlikely to be able to pursue collection from you for the debt unless your spouse used them for the necessities of life, such as food, necessary clothing, or housing.

13.7 During our marriage, we paid off thousands of dollars of debt incurred by my spouse before we were married. Will the court take this into consideration when dividing our property and debt?

It might. Just as premarital assets can have an impact on the overall division of property and debts, so can premarital debt. Depending upon the length of the marriage, the evidence of the debt, and the amount paid, it may be a factor for the judge to consider.

Be sure to let your attorney know if either you or your spouse brought substantial debt into the marriage.

13.8 Regarding debts, what is a *hold-harmless clause,* and why should it be in the divorce decree?

A *hold-harmless* provision is intended to protect you in the event that your spouse fails to follow a court order to pay a debt after the divorce is granted. The language typically provides that your spouse shall "indemnify and hold [you] harmless from liability" on the debt.

If you and your spouse have a joint debt and your spouse fails to pay, the creditor may nevertheless attempt to collect from you. This is because the court is without power to change the creditor's rights and can make orders affecting only you and your spouse.

In the event your spouse fails to pay a court-ordered debt and the creditor attempts collection from you, the hold-harmless provision in your divorce decree can be used in an effort to insist that payment is made by your former spouse.

13.9 My spouse and I have agreed that I will keep our home; why must I refinance the mortgage?

There may be a number of reasons why your spouse is asking you to refinance the mortgage. First, the mortgage company cannot be forced to take your spouse's name off of the mortgage note. This means that if you did not make the house payments, the lender could pursue collection against your spouse.

Second, your spouse may want to receive his or her share of the home equity. It may be possible for you to borrow additional money at the time of refinancing to pay your spouse his or her share of the equity in the home.

Third, the mortgage on your family home may prevent your spouse from buying a home in the future. Because there remains a risk that your spouse could be pursued for the debt to the mortgage company, it is unlikely that a second lender will want to take the risk of extending further credit to your spouse.

13.10 Can I file for bankruptcy while my divorce is pending?

Yes. Consult with your attorney if you are considering filing for bankruptcy while your divorce is pending. It will be important for you to ask yourself a number of questions, such as:

- Should I file for bankruptcy on my own or with my spouse?
- How will filing for bankruptcy affect my ability to purchase a home in the future?
- Which debts can be discharged in bankruptcy, and which cannot?

- How will a bankruptcy affect the division of property and debts in the divorce?
- How might a delay in the divorce proceeding due to a bankruptcy impact my case?
- What form of bankruptcy is best for my situation?

If you use a different attorney for your bankruptcy than you have for your divorce, be sure that each attorney is kept fully informed about the developments in the other case.

13.11 What happens if my spouse files for bankruptcy during our divorce?

Contact your attorney right away. The filing of a bankruptcy while your divorce is pending can have a significant impact on your divorce. Your attorney can advise you whether certain debts are likely to be discharged in the bankruptcy, the delay a bankruptcy may cause to your divorce, and whether bankruptcy is an appropriate option for you.

13.12 Can I file for divorce while I am in bankruptcy?

Yes, however, you must receive the bankruptcy court's permission to proceed with the divorce. Although in bankruptcy, your property is protected from debt collection by the *automatic stay*. The stay can also prevent the divorce court from dividing property between you and your spouse until you obtain the bankruptcy court's permission to proceed with the divorce.

13.13 What should I do if my former spouse files for bankruptcy after our divorce?

Contact your attorney immediately. If you learn that your former spouse has filed for bankruptcy, you may have certain rights to object to the discharge of any debts your spouse was ordered to pay under your divorce decree. If you fail to take action, it is possible that you will be held responsible for debts your spouse was ordered to pay.

13.14 If I am awarded child support or alimony in my decree, can these obligations be discharged if my former spouse files for bankruptcy after our divorce?

No, support obligations such as child support and alimony are not dischargeable in bankruptcy, meaning these debts cannot be eliminated in a bankruptcy proceeding.

13.15 What happens if my former spouse does not pay his or her obligations in the decree?

If your former spouse does not pay the debts assigned to him or her in the decree, you may be able to pursue a contempt of court action. A party is in contempt of court if he or she willfully disobeys or disregards a court order. Talk with your attorney to determine whether a contempt of court action may be filed in your case to enforce your rights under your decree.

14

Taxes

Nobody likes a surprise letter from the Internal Revenue Service saying he or she owes more taxes. When your divorce is over, you want to be sure that you don't later discover you owe taxes you weren't expecting to pay.

A number of tax issues may arise in your divorce. Your attorney may not be able to answer all of your tax questions, so consulting your accountant or tax advisor for additional advice might be necessary.

Taxes are important considerations in both settlement negotiations and trial preparation. They should not be overlooked. Taxes can impact many of your decisions, including those regarding alimony, division of property, and the receipt of benefits.

Be sure to ask the professionals helping you about the tax implications in your divorce so you don't get a letter in the mail that begins, "Dear Taxpayer: ...."

14.1 Will either my spouse or I have to pay income tax when we transfer property or pay a property settlement to each other according to our divorce decree?

No. However, it is important that you see the future tax consequences of a subsequent withdrawal, sale, or transfer of certain assets you receive in your divorce.

It is important to ask your attorney to take tax consequences into consideration when looking at the division of your assets.

14.2   Is the amount of child support I pay tax deductible?

No.

14.3   Do I have to pay income tax on any child support I receive?

No. Your child support is tax free regardless of when it is paid or when it is received.

14.4   What does the IRS consider alimony?

Amounts paid under a divorce decree or pursuant to a written separation agreement entered into between you and your spouse will be considered alimony if:

- You and your spouse or former spouse do not file a joint return with each other.
- The payment is in cash (including checks or money orders).
- The payment is received by (or on behalf of) your spouse or former spouse.
- You and your former spouse are not members of the same household when you make the payment.
- You have no liability to make the payment (in cash or property) after the death of your spouse or former spouse.
- Your payment is not treated as child support or a property settlement.

Thus, not all payments made according to a divorce or separation decree are alimony. Alimony does not include:

- Child support
- Noncash property settlements
- Payments to keep up the payer's property
- Use of the payer's property

14.5   Is the amount of alimony I am ordered to pay tax deductible?

Yes. Spousal support paid pursuant to a court order is deductible. This will include court-ordered alimony and may also include other forms of support provided to your former spouse (but not child support). Your tax deduction is a factor to consider when determining a fair amount of alimony to be paid in your case.

14.6   Do I have to pay tax on the alimony I receive?

Yes. You must pay income tax on the spousal support you receive. This will include court-ordered alimony and may also include other forms of spousal support, but not child support, paid by your spouse.

Income tax is a critical factor in determining a fair amount of alimony. Insist that your attorney bring this issue to the attention of your spouse's lawyer, or to the judge, if your case proceeds to trial so that both the tax you pay and the deduction your spouse receives are taken into consideration.

Be sure to consult with your tax advisor about payment of tax on your spousal support. Making estimated tax payments throughout the year or withholding additional taxes from your wages can avoid a burdensome tax liability at the end of the year.

It is important to budget for payment of tax on your alimony. Taxes are another item to consider when looking at your monthly living expenses for the purposes of seeking an alimony award.

14.7   Is there anything else I should know about alimony and taxes?

If your alimony payments to your spouse decrease or end during the first three calendar years after your divorce, you may be subject to the *recapture rule*. You are subject to the recapture rule if the alimony you pay in the third year decreases by more than $15,000 from the second year or alimony you pay in the second and third year decreases significantly from the alimony you pay in the first year. If you are subject to this rule, you must claim a portion of the alimony payments you've previously deducted as income in the third year. Likewise, the recipient can deduct part of the alimony payments he or she previously claimed as income in the third year.

Taxes

14.8 During the divorce proceedings, is our tax filing status affected?

It can be. You are considered unmarried if your decree is final by December 31 of the tax year. Under Michigan law, your decree becomes final for tax purposes thirty days after it is entered by the court.

If you are considered unmarried, your filing status is either "single" or, under certain circumstances, "head of household." If your decree is not final as of December 31, your filing status is either "married filing a joint return" or "married filing a separate return," unless you live apart from your spouse and meet the exception for "head of household."

While your divorce is in progress, talk to both your tax advisor and your attorney about your filing status. It may be beneficial to figure your tax on both a joint return and a separate return to see which gives you the lower tax. IRS Publication 504, Divorced or Separated Individuals, provides more detail on tax issues while you are going through a divorce.

14.9 Should I file a joint income tax return with my spouse while our divorce is pending?

Consult your tax advisor to determine the risks and benefits of filing a joint return with your spouse. Compare this with the consequences of filing your tax return separately. Often the overall tax liability will be less with the filing of a joint return, but other factors are important to consider.

When deciding whether to file a joint return with your spouse, consider any concerns you have about the accuracy and truthfulness of the information on the tax return. If you have any doubts, consult both your attorney and your tax advisor before agreeing to sign a joint tax return with your spouse. Prior to filing a return with your spouse, try to reach agreement about how any tax owed or refund expected will be shared, and ask your lawyer to assist you in getting this in writing.

14.10 My spouse will not cooperate in providing the necessary documents to prepare or file our taxes jointly. What options do I have?

Talk with your attorney about requesting your spouse to cooperate in the preparation and filing of your joint return. Although a judge cannot order your spouse to sign a joint return,

165

he or she can penalize your spouse for his or her unreasonable refusal to do so.

14.11 For tax purposes, is one time of year better to divorce than another?

It depends upon your tax situation. If you and your spouse agree that it would be beneficial to file joint tax returns for the year in which you are divorcing, you may wish to not have your divorce finalized before the end of the year.

Your marital status for filing income taxes is determined by your status on December 31. Consequently, if you both want to preserve your right to file a joint return, your decree should not be entered before December 1 of that year.

14.12 What tax consequences should I consider regarding the sale of our home?

When your home is sold, whether during your divorce or after, the sale may be subject to a *capital gains tax.* If your home was your primary residence and you lived in the home for two of the preceding five years, you may be eligible to exclude up to $250,000 of the gain on the sale of your home. If both you and your spouse meet the ownership and residence tests, you may be eligible to exclude up to $500,000 of the gain.

If you anticipate the gain on the sale of your residence to be over $250,000, talk with your attorney early in the divorce process about a plan to minimize the tax liability. For more information, see IRS Publication 523, Selling Your Home, or visit the IRS website at www.irs.gov and talk with your tax advisor.

14.13 How might capital gains tax be a problem for me years after the divorce?

Future capital gains tax on the sale of property should be discussed with your attorney during the negotiation and trial preparation stages of your case. This is especially important if the sale of the property is imminent. Failure to do so may result in an unfair outcome.

For example, suppose you agree that your spouse will be awarded the proceeds from the sale of your home valued at $200,000, after the real estate commission, and you will take the stock portfolio also valued at $200,000.

Taxes

Suppose that after the divorce, you decide to sell the stock. It is still valued at $200,000, but you learn that its original price was $120,000 and that you must pay capital gains tax of 15 percent on the $80,000 of gain. You pay tax of $12,000, leaving you with $188,000.

Meanwhile, your former spouse sells the marital home but pays no capital gains tax because he qualifies for the $250,000 exemption. He is left with the full $200,000.

Tax implications of your property division should always be discussed with your attorney, with support from your tax advisor as needed.

14.14 During and after the divorce, who gets to claim the children as dependents?

This issue should be addressed in settlement negotiations or at trial, if settlement is not reached.

The judge has discretion to determine which parent will be entitled to claim the children as exemptions for income tax purposes. Where child support has been ordered pursuant to the Michigan Child Support Guidelines, many judges order that the exemptions be shared or alternated. However, most judges will order that the payor of child support be current on his or her child-support obligation to be eligible to claim the income tax dependency exemption. Additionally, if one party has income so low or so high that he or she will not benefit from the dependency exemption, the court may award the exemption to the other parent.

14.15 My decree says I have to sign IRS Form 8332 so my former spouse can claim our child as an exemption, because I have custody. Should I sign it once for all future years?

No. Child custody and child support can be modified in the future. If there is a future modification of custody or support, which parent is entitled to claim your child as an exemption could change. The best practice is to provide your former spouse a timely copy of Form 8332 (Release/Revocation of Release of Claim to Exemption for Child by Custodial Parent), signed by you for the appropriate tax year only.

14.16 Can my spouse and I split the child-care tax credit?

According to the Michigan child-support guidelines, the value of the federal income tax credit for child care must be considered when determining the payor spouse's obligation to contribute to child-care expenses.

The value of the federal child-care tax credit must be subtracted from the actual costs of child care to arrive at a figure for net child-care expenses owed by the spouse paying support.

Only the custodial parent is allowed to claim the credit. If you are a noncustodial parent and paying child care, talk to your lawyer about how to address this issue in your divorce decree.

14.17 Do I have to pay taxes on the portion of my spouse's 401(k) that was awarded to me in the divorce?

If you have been awarded a portion of your former spouse's 401(k) or 403(b) retirement plan, any distribution of these funds to you will be subject to regular income tax. However, it may be possible for you to elect to receive all or a portion of these assets without incurring the 10 percent early-withdrawal penalty (applicable if you are under age 59½) if you decide to take the money rather than keep an account in your name or roll over the assets to an IRA or other permitted retirement account. Talk with your attorney and your tax advisor to determine your options.

14.18 Is the cost of getting a divorce, including my attorney fees, tax deductible under any circumstances?

Your legal fees for getting a divorce are not deductible. However, a portion of your attorney fees may be deductible if they are for:

- The production of taxable income, such as alimony or interest income
- Advice regarding the determination of taxes or tax due

Attorney fees are "miscellaneous" deductions for individuals and are consequently limited to 2 percent of your adjusted gross income. More details can be found in IRS Publication 529, Miscellaneous Deductions.

You may also be able to deduct fees you pay to appraisers or accountants who help. Talk to your tax advisor about whether any portion of your attorney fees or other expenses from your divorce is deductible.

14.19 Do I have to complete a new Form W-4 for my employer because of my divorce?

Completing a new Form W-4, Employee's Withholding Certificate, will help you to claim the proper withholding allowances based upon your marital status and exemptions. Also, if you are receiving alimony, you may need to make quarterly estimated tax payments. Consult with your tax advisor to ensure you are making the most preferable tax planning decision.

14.20 What is *innocent spouse relief,* and how can it help me?

Innocent spouse relief refers to a method of obtaining relief from the Internal Revenue Service for taxes owed as a result of a joint income tax return filed during your marriage. Numerous factors affect your eligibility for innocent spouse tax relief, such as:

- You would suffer a financial hardship if you were required to pay the tax.
- You did not significantly benefit from the unpaid taxes.
- You suffered abuse during your marriage.
- You thought your spouse would pay the taxes on the original return.

Talk with your attorney or your tax advisor if you are concerned about liability for taxes arising from joint tax returns filed during the marriage. You may benefit from a referral to an attorney who specializes in tax law.

15

Going to Court

For many of us, our images of going to court are created by movie scenes and our favorite television shows. We picture the witness breaking down in tears after a grueling cross-examination. We see lawyers strutting around the courtroom, waving their arms as they plead their case to the jury.

Hollywood drama, however, is a far cry from reality. Going to court for your divorce can mean many things, ranging from sitting in a hallway while waiting for the lawyers and judges to conclude a conference, to being on the witness standing giving mundane answers to questions about your monthly living expenses.

Regardless of the nature of your court proceeding, going to court often evokes a sense of anxiety. Perhaps your divorce might be the first time in your life that you have even been in a courtroom. Be assured that these feelings of nervousness and uncertainty are normal.

Understanding what will occur in court and being well prepared for any court hearings will relieve much of your stress. Knowing the order of events, the role of the people in the courtroom, etiquette in the courtroom, and what is expected of you will make the entire experience easier.

Your lawyer will be with you at all times to support you any time you go to court. Remember, every court appearance moves you one step closer to completing your divorce so that you can move forward with your life.

15.1 What do I need to know about appearing in court and court dates in general?

Court dates are important. As soon as you receive a notice from your attorney about a court date in your case, confirm whether your attendance will be required and put it on your calendar.

Ask your attorney about the nature of the hearing, including whether the judge will be listening to testimony by witnesses, reading affidavits, or merely listening to the arguments of the lawyers.

Ask whether it is necessary for you to meet with your attorney or take any other action to prepare for the hearing, such as providing additional information or documents.

Find out how long the hearing is expected to last. It may be as short as a few minutes or as long as a day or more.

If you plan to attend the hearing, determine where and when to meet your attorney. Depending upon the type of hearing, your lawyer may want you to arrive in advance of the scheduled hearing time to prepare.

Make sure you know the location of the courthouse, where to park, and the floor and room number of the courtroom. Planning for such simple matters as having change for a parking meter can eliminate unnecessary stress. If you want someone to go to court with you to provide you support, check with your attorney first.

15.2 When and how often will I need to go to court?

Whether and how often you will need to go to court depends upon a number of factors. Depending upon the complexity of your case, you may have only one hearing or numerous court hearings throughout the course of your divorce.

Some hearings, usually those on procedural matters, are attended only by the attorneys. These could include requests for the other side to provide information or for the setting of certain deadlines. These hearings are often brief and held in the judge's chambers rather than in the courtroom. Other hearings, such as temporary hearings for custody or support, are typically attended by both parties and their attorneys.

If you and your spouse settle all of the issues in your case, although not required, you can choose to testify at a final hearing in which the judge will review and approve your decree.

If your case proceeds to trial, your appearance will be required for the duration of the trial. In Michigan, divorce matters are heard before a judge only; juries do not hear divorces.

15.3 How much notice will I receive about appearing in court?

The amount of notice you will receive for any court hearing can vary from a few days to several weeks. Ask your attorney whether and when it will be necessary for you to appear in court on your case so that you can have ease in preparing and planning.

If you receive a notice of a hearing, contact your attorney immediately. He or she can tell you whether your appearance is required and what other steps are needed to prepare.

15.4 I am afraid to be alone in the same room with my spouse. When I go to court, is this going to happen if the lawyers go into the judge's office to discuss the case?

Talk to your lawyer. Prior to any court hearing, you and your spouse may be asked to wait while your attorneys meet with the judge to discuss preliminary matters.

A number of options are likely to be available to ensure that you feel safe. These might include having you and your spouse wait in different locations or having a friend or family member present.

Your lawyer wants to support you in feeling secure throughout all court proceedings. Just let him or her know your concerns.

15.5 Do I have to go to court every time there is a court hearing on any motion?

Not necessarily. Some matters will be decided by the judge after listening to the arguments of the lawyers. These hearings are sometimes held in the judge's office, referred to as *chambers*, and you will not be required to attend.

15.6 My spouse's lawyer keeps asking for *adjournments of court dates*. Is there anything I can do to stop this?

Adjournments of court dates are not unusual in divorces. A court date might be postponed for many reasons, including a conflict on the calendar of one of the attorneys or the judge, the lack of availability of one of the parties or an important witness, or the need for more time to prepare.

Discuss with your attorney your desire to move your case forward without further delay so that repeated requests for continuances can be resisted.

15.7 If I have to go to court, will I be put on the stand? Will there be a jury?

In Michigan, divorce matters are heard before a judge only; juries do not hear divorces. Whether you will be put on the stand will depend upon the nature of the issues in dispute, the judge assigned to your case, and your attorney's strategy for your case.

15.8 My lawyer said I need to be in court for our *status conference* next week. What's going to happen?

A *status conference*, also called a *settlement conference*, is held to determine a schedule for your divorce matter, including important dates such as a deadline for mediation and trial dates; to determine a mediator to mediate your case; and to provide the judge an opportunity to check in with the parties and attorneys and determine which subjects are at issue in your divorce matter.

Although you should plan to attend your status conference, it is possible that the hearing will be held in the judge's chambers with only the judge and attorneys present.

Even if your status conference is held in the judge's chambers, your presence at the hearing is still important. Your attorney may need additional information from you during the hearing and often the judge wishes you to be present to hear the scheduling and procedural details that will be discussed.

15.9 My attorney said I need to be in court for our temporary hearing. What will occur?

A temporary hearing is held to determine such matters as who remains in the house while your divorce is pending, temporary physical custody of the children, temporary support, and other financial matters.

The procedure for your temporary hearing can vary depending upon the county in which your case was filed, the judge to which the case is assigned, and whether or not temporary custody is disputed.

Even if testimony is not taken at your temporary hearing, your presence is still important. Your attorney may need additional information from you during the hearing, and last-minute negotiations to resolve temporary issues are not uncommon.

In some counties, your hearing will be one of numerous other hearings on the judge's calendar. You may find yourself in a courtroom with many other attorneys and their clients, all having matters scheduled before the court that day. Even though you are present in the courtroom, your attorney will make your argument to the judge, and it is unlikely you will be required to provide formal testimony.

If temporary custody is disputed, you and other witnesses might be required to take the witness stand to give testimony at your temporary hearing. If this is the case, meeting with your attorney in advance to fully prepare is very important.

Talk to your attorney about the procedure you should expect for the temporary hearing in your case.

15.10 Do I have to go to court if all of the issues in my case are settled?

It depends. If you are the plaintiff (the one who filed the case) in your divorce matter, you will be required to attend a final hearing during which your attorney will ask you questions relating to the agreements you and your spouse reached and other simple, but mandatory, questions regarding your complaint for divorce. Your attorney will prepare you for these questions prior to the hearing. At this hearing, the judge will review and approve your decree and may ask you a few questions as well.

15.11 Are there any rules about courtroom etiquette that I need to know?

Knowing a few tips about being in the courtroom will make your experience easier.

- Dress appropriately. Avoid overly casual dress, lots of jewelry, revealing clothing, and extreme hairstyles.
- Don't bring beverages into the courtroom. Most courts have rules that do not allow food and drink in courtrooms. If you need water, ask your lawyer.
- Dispose of chewing gum before giving testimony.
- Don't talk aloud in the courtroom unless you're on the witness stand or being questioned by the judge.
- Do not enter the judge's office.
- Stand up whenever the judge is entering or leaving the courtroom.
- Be sure to turn off your electronic devices.
- Be mindful that the judge may be observing you and those you bring to the hearing at all times.

Although you may feel anxious initially, you'll likely feel more relaxed about the courtroom setting once your hearing gets underway.

15.12 What is the role of the *court clerk*?

The *court clerk* provides support for the judge and lawyers in the management of the court calendar and the courtroom. He or she assists in the scheduling of court hearings and the management of legal documents given to the judge for review, such as temporary orders and divorce decrees.

15.13 Will there be a *court reporter,* and what will he or she do?

A *court reporter* is a professional trained to make an accurate record of the words spoken and documents offered into evidence during court proceedings. Some counties use tape or video recording devices rather than court reporters.

A written transcript of a court proceeding may be purchased from the court reporter. If your case is appealed, the transcript prepared by the court reporter will be used by the appeals court to review the facts of your case.

The court reporter is also responsible for managing documents and other items offered into evidence at trial.

Some hearings are held *off the record,* which means that the court reporter is not making a record of what is being said. Ordinarily, these are matters for which no appeal is expected to be taken.

15.14 Will I be able to talk to my attorney while we are in court?

During court proceedings it is important that your attorney give his or her attention to anything being said by the judge, witnesses, or your spouse's lawyer. For this reason, your attorney will avoid talking with you when anyone else in the courtroom is speaking.

Plan to have pen and paper with you when you go to court. If your court proceeding is underway and your lawyer is listening to what is being said by others in the courtroom, write him or her a note with your questions or comments.

It is critical that your attorney hear each question asked by the other lawyer and all answers given by each witness. If not, opportunities for making objections to inappropriate evidence may be lost. You can support your attorney in doing an effective job for you by avoiding talking to him or her while a court hearing is in progress.

If your court hearing is lengthy, breaks will be taken. You can use this time to discuss with your attorney any questions or observations you have about the proceeding.

15.15 What questions might my lawyer ask me about the problems in our marriage and why I want the divorce?

Because Michigan is a no-fault state, your lawyer will ask you questions to show the court that the marriage is irretrievably broken, without going into detail about the specific difficulties in your marriage.

The only question required by law is:

Attorney: "Has there been a breakdown of the marriage relationship to the extent that the objects of matrimony have been destroyed and there remains no reasonable likelihood the marriage can be preserved?"

To which you answer: "Yes."

Your attorney may also ask:

Attorney: "If the judge did not grant you a divorce, would you ever reside with your husband again as husband and wife?"

You would answer: "No."

It is unlikely that you will be asked in great detail about the nature of the marital problems that led to the divorce. In the majority of cases, questions like those just mentioned will satisfy the judge that the requirements under Michigan law for the dissolving of a marriage have been met.

15.16 My lawyer said that the judge has issued a *scheduling order* having to do with my upcoming trial and that we'll have to comply with it. What does this mean?

Ask your lawyer for a copy of the *scheduling order.* Judges will order that certain information be provided either to the opposing party or to the judge by certain dates, in advance of trial. This might include:

- A list of issues that have been settled
- A list of issues that are still disputed
- Agreements, referred to as *stipulations,* as to the truth of certain facts
- The names of witnesses
- Exhibits
- A summary of how you want the judge to decide the case
- Deadlines for providing the information

15.17 What is a *pretrial conference*?

A *pretrial conference* is a meeting held with the lawyers and the judge to review information related to an upcoming trial, such as:

- How long the trial is expected to last
- The issues in dispute
- The law surrounding the disputed issues
- The identification of witnesses
- Trial exhibits
- The status of negotiations

Divorce in Michigan

Often a firm trial date is set at the pretrial conference, meaning the judge will not grant an adjournment of that date absent some unforeseen circumstances. If a pretrial conference is held in your case, ask your attorney whether you should attend. Your attorney may request that you either be present for the conference or be available by phone.

15.18 Besides meeting with my lawyer, is there anything else I should do to prepare for my upcoming trial?

Yes. Be sure to review your deposition and any information you provided in your discovery, such as answers to interrogatories. Also be sure to review any affidavits previously submitted to the judge. At trial, it is possible that you will be asked some of the same questions. If you think you might give different answers at trial, discuss this with your lawyer.

It is important that your attorney know in advance of trial whether any information you provided during the discovery process has changed.

15.19 I'm meeting with my lawyer to prepare for trial. How do I make the most of these meetings?

Meeting with your lawyer to prepare for your trial is important to achieving a good outcome. Come to the meeting prepared to discuss the following:

- The issues in your case
- Your desired outcome on each of the issues
- The questions you might be asked at trial by both lawyers
- The exhibits that will be offered into evidence during the trial
- The witnesses for your trial
- The status of negotiations

Your meeting with your lawyer will help you better understand what to expect at your trial and make the trial experience easier.

15.20 My lawyer says that the law firm is busy with *trial preparation*. What exactly is my lawyer doing to prepare for my trial?

Countless tasks are necessary to perform to prepare your case for trial. These are just some of them:

- Developing arguments to be made on each of the contested issues
- Researching and reviewing the relevant law in your case
- Reviewing the facts of your case to determine which witnesses are best suited to testifying about them
- Reviewing, selecting, and preparing exhibits
- Preparing questions for all witnesses
- Preparing an opening statement
- Reviewing rules on evidence to prepare for any objections to make or oppose at trial
- Determining the order of witnesses and all exhibits
- Preparing your file for the day in court, including preparing a trial notebook with essential information

Your lawyer is committed to a good outcome for you in your divorce. He or she will be engaged in many important actions to fully prepare your case for trial.

15.21 How do I know who my witnesses will be at trial?

Well in advance of your trial date, your lawyer will discuss with you whether other witnesses, besides you and your spouse, will be necessary. Witnesses can include family members, friends, child-care providers, and clergy members. When thinking of potential witnesses, consider your relationship with the witness, whether that witness has had an opportunity to observe relevant facts, and whether the witness has knowledge different from that of other witnesses. For more information on identifying potential witnesses, please *see* question 8.18 in chapter 8.

You may also have expert witnesses testify on your behalf. An expert witness will provide opinion testimony based upon specialized knowledge, training, or experience. For example, a psychologist, real estate appraiser, or accountant may provide expert testimony on your behalf.

15.22 My divorce is scheduled for trial. Does this mean there is no hope for a settlement?

Many cases are settled after a trial date is set. The setting of a trial date may cause you and your spouse to think about the risks and costs of going to trial. This can help you and your spouse focus on what is most important to you and lead you toward a negotiated settlement. Because the costs of preparing for and proceeding to trial are substantial, it is best to engage in settlement negotiations well in advance of your trial date. However, it is not uncommon for cases to settle a few days before trial, or even at the courthouse before your trial begins.

15.23 Can I prevent my spouse from being in the courtroom?

Probably not. Because your spouse has a legal interest in the outcome of your divorce, he or she has a right to be present. Michigan courtrooms are open to the public. Consequently, it is not uncommon for persons not involved in your divorce to pass through the courtroom at various times simply because they have other business with the court.

15.24 Can I take a friend or family member with me to court?

Yes. Let your attorney know in advance if you intend to bring anyone to court with you. Some people important to you may be very emotional about your divorce or your spouse. Be sure to invite someone who is better able to focus attention on supporting you rather than on his or her own feelings.

15.25 Can my friends and family be present in the courtroom during my trial?

It depends upon whether they will be witnesses in your case. In most cases where witnesses other than the husband and wife are testifying, the attorneys request that the court *sequester* the witnesses. The judge would then order all witnesses, except you and your spouse, to leave the courtroom until after they have testified.

Once a witness has completed his or her testimony, he or she will ordinarily be allowed to remain in the courtroom for the remainder of the trial.

15.26 I want to do a great job testifying as a witness in my divorce trial. What are some tips?

Keep the following in mind to be a good witness on your own behalf:

- Tell the truth. Although this may not be always be comfortable, it is critical if you want your testimony to be believed by the judge.

- Listen carefully to the complete question before thinking of your answer. Wait to consider your answer until the full question is asked.

- Slow down. It's easy to speed up our speech when we are anxious. Taking your time with your answers ensures that the judge hears you and that the court reporter can accurately record your testimony.

- If you don't understand a question or don't know the answer, be sure to say so.

- If the question calls for a "yes" or "no" answer, simply say so. Then wait for the attorney to ask you the next question. If there is more you want to explain, remember that you have already told your attorney all the important facts and he or she will make sure you are allowed to give any testimony significant in your case.

- Don't argue with the judge or the lawyers.

- Take your time. You may be asked some questions that call for a thoughtful response. If you need a moment to reflect on an answer before you give it, allow yourself that time.

- Stop speaking if an objection is made by one of the lawyers. Wait until the judge has decided whether to allow you to answer.

- If you begin to feel emotional, your lawyer can ask for a short break.

15.27 Should I be worried about being cross-examined by my spouse's lawyer at trial?

If your case goes to trial, prepare to be asked some questions by your spouse's lawyer. Many of these questions will call for a simple "yes" or "no."

If you are worried about particular questions, discuss your concerns with your attorney. He or she can support you in giving a truthful response. Focus on preparing well for being asked questions by your spouse's lawyer. Try not to take the questions personally; remember that the lawyer is fulfilling a duty to advocate for your spouse's interests. Remember that you are just doing your best to tell the truth about the facts.

15.28 What happens on the day of trial?

Although no two trials are alike, the following steps will occur in most divorce trials:

- Attorneys meet with the judge in chambers to discuss procedural issues, such as how many witnesses will be called, how long the case will take to present, and when breaks might be taken.
- Attorneys give opening statements.
- Plaintiff's attorney calls plaintiff's witnesses to testify.
- Defendant's attorney may cross-examine each of them.
- Defendant's attorney calls defendant's witnesses to testify.
- Plaintiff's attorney may cross-examine each of them.
- Plaintiff's lawyer calls any *rebuttal witnesses,* that is, witnesses whose testimony contradicts the testimony of the defendant's witnesses.
- Closing arguments are made first by the plaintiff's attorney and then by the defendant's attorney.

15.29 Will the judge decide my case the day I go to court?

No. There is so much information from the trial for the judge to consider that it is not possible for the judge to give an immediate ruling.

The judge may want to review documents, review the law, perform calculations, review his or her notes, and give thoughtful consideration to the issues to be decided. For this reason, it may be days, weeks, or, in some cases, even longer before a ruling is made.

When a judge does not make a ruling immediately upon the conclusion of a trial, it is said that the case has been *taken under advisement.*

16

The Appeals Process

You may find that, despite your best efforts to settle your case, your divorce went to trial and the judge made major decisions that will have a serious impact on your future. You may be either gravely disappointed or even shocked by the judge's ruling.

The judge might have seen your case differently than you and your attorney did. Perhaps the judge made mistakes. Or it may be that Michigan law simply does not allow for the outcome you were hoping for.

Whatever the reasons for the court's rulings, you may feel that the judge's decisions are not ones that you can live with. If this is the case, talk to your lawyer immediately about your right to appeal. Together you can decide whether an appeal is in your best interests, or whether it is better to accept the court's ruling and invest your energy in moving forward with your future without an appeal.

16.1 How much time after my divorce do I have to file an appeal?

You must file an appeal within thirty days of the final order you wish to appeal. Because your attorney may also recommend filing certain motions following your trial, discuss your appeal rights with your lawyer as soon as you have received the judge's ruling.

A timely discussion with your attorney about your right to appeal is essential so important deadlines are not missed.

16.2   Can I appeal a temporary order?

Yes. Under Michigan law, temporary orders may be appealed.

16.3   What parts of the decree can be appealed?

If you or your spouse is unhappy with final decisions made by the judge in your case, either of you can file an appeal. Decisions that can be appealed include custody, parenting time, child support, alimony, division of property, and attorney's fees.

16.4   Will my attorney recommend I appeal specific aspects of the decree, or will I have to request it?

Your attorney may counsel you to file an appeal on certain issues of your case; you may also ask your lawyer whether there is a legitimate basis for an appeal of any decision you believe is wrong. Talk to your attorney regarding the decisions most dissatisfying to you. Your lawyer can advise which issues have the greatest likelihood of success on appeal, in light of the facts of your case and Michigan law.

16.5   When should an appeal be filed?

An appeal should be filed only after careful consultation with your lawyer when you believe that the judge has made a serious error under the law or the facts of your case. Among the factors you and your attorney should discuss are:

- Whether the judge had the authority under the law to make the decisions set forth in your decree
- The likelihood of the success of your appeal
- The risk that an appeal by you will encourage an appeal by your former spouse
- The cost of the appeal
- The length of time an appeal can be expected to take
- The impact of a delay in the case during the appeal

The deadline for filing an appeal is thirty days from the date that a final order is entered in your case. It is important that you are clear about the deadline that applies in your case, so talk to your attorney at once if you are thinking about an appeal.

16.6   Are there any disadvantages to filing an appeal?

There can be disadvantages to filing an appeal, including:

- Uncertainty as to the outcome
- Increase in attorney's fees and costs
- The risks of a worse outcome on appeal than you received at trial
- Delay
- Prolonged conflict between you and your former spouse
- Risk of a second trial occurring after the appeal
- Difficulty in obtaining closure and moving forward with your life

16.7   Is an attorney necessary to appeal?

The appeals process is very detailed and specific, with set deadlines and specific court rules. Given the complex nature of the appellate process, you should have an attorney if you intend to file an appeal.

16.8   How long does the appeals process usually take?

It depends. An appeal can take anywhere from several months to well over a year. An appeal may also result in the appellate court requiring further proceedings by the trial court. This will result in further delay.

16.9   What are the steps in the appeals process?

There are many steps that your lawyer will take on your behalf in the appeal process, including:

- Identifying the issues to be appealed
- Filing a notice with the court of your intent to appeal
- Obtaining the necessary court documents and trial exhibits to send to the appellate court
- Obtaining a transcript of the trial, as well as a written copy of testimony by witnesses and statements by the judge and the lawyers made in the presence of the court reporter
- Performing legal research to support your arguments on appeal

- Preparing and filing a document known as a *brief,* which sets forth the facts of the case and relevant law, complete with citations to the court transcripts, court documents, and prior cases
- Making an oral argument before the judges of the appellate court

16.10 Is filing and pursuing an appeal expensive?

Yes. In addition to filing fees and lawyer fees, there is likely to be a substantial cost for the preparation of the transcript of the trial testimony.

16.11 If I do not file an appeal, can I ever go back to court to change my decree?

Certain aspects of a decree are not modifiable, such as the division of property and debts or the award of attorney fees. Other parts of your decree, such as support or matters regarding the children, may be modified if there has been a "material and substantial change in circumstances."

A modification of custody or parenting time for minor children will also require you to show that the change would be in their best interests.

If your decree did not provide for alimony or if it ordered that the alimony be nonmodifiable, it is unlikely that you will have any basis for a modification. If you believe that you have a basis for a modification of your divorce decree, consult with your attorney.

In Closing

Now, pause and breathe. Acknowledge yourself for the courage you have shown in examining your unique situation, needs, and goals. Now, you are facing your future—recasting yourself into a new life. You are looking more closely at your living situation, the needs of your children, your financial security, and your personal growth and healing. You are seeing your situation clearly and being honest with yourself about what you now need. You are taking action to propel yourself into new possibilities.

From here, it is time to take inventory of the lessons learned, goals met, and action yet to take. Celebrate each of those steps forward and be gentle with yourself over the occasional misstep backward. You have transitioned through this time when everything is reduced to the core of you. Gone are the familiar habits of your marriage. With every day moving closer to the completion of your divorce, your grief will begin to subside and your energy improve as you move toward a fresh start.

All the best to you as you accomplish this life journey!

Appendix

Sample Complaint for Divorce
—including *Ex parte* Orders

STATE OF MICHIGAN
IN THE CIRCUIT COURT FOR THE COUNTY OF_____.

_____	)	
Plaintiff,	)	
	)	
vs.	)	**Case No.**
	)	**HON.**
_____	)	_____
Defendant.	)	

COMPLAINT FOR DIVORCE
AND PETITION FOR *EX PARTE* RELIEF

NOW COMES_____, Plaintiff herein by _____, his attorneys, and for his *Complaint for Divorce and Petition for Ex Parte Relief,* he submits unto this honorable Court as follows:

1.   Plaintiff has resided in the County of _____for more than ten (10) days immediately preceding the filing of this Complaint for Divorce. Plaintiff has resided in the State of Michigan for more than 180 days immediately preceding the filing of this Complaint for Divorce. Plaintiff is domiciled in the State of Michigan at the time of the filing of this Complaint for Divorce.

2.   On or about the _____ day of_____, _____, in [City], [State], Plaintiff was duly and legally married to_____, Defendant

Sample Complaint for Divorce (Continued)

herein, by a minister duly and legally authorized to solemnize marriages, and the parties thereafter lived and cohabited together as husband and wife.

3. The name of the wife prior to said marriage was _____.

4. During and as a result of said marriage, and up to the date of filing this Complaint for Divorce, _____ (_) child(ren) were born to the parties hereto: _____born on _____(age __).

5. In accordance with the best interests of the parties' minor child(ren), the parties should share joint legal custody, and Plaintiff should be awarded physical custody of the parties' minor child(ren), with reasonable parenting time to Defendant.

6. Pursuant to MCLA 600.659, MSA 27A.659, Plaintiff states:

    a. The minor child(ren) presently reside with the parties at _____, [City], [State], and they have resided with the parties throughout their life;

    b. Plaintiff is not aware of any other litigation involving the minor child(ren), and Plaintiff has not participated in any capacity in other litigation concerning custody of the minor child(ren) in a court of this or another state;

    c. Plaintiff has no information of a custody proceeding concerning these minor child(ren) in a court of this or any other state; and

    d. Plaintiff does not know of any person not a party to these proceedings who has physical custody of the same child(ren) or claims custody or parenting time rights with these minor child(ren).

7. To the best of Plaintiff's information and belief, Defendant is not pregnant.

8. There has been a breakdown of the marriage relationship to the extent that the objects of matrimony have been destroyed and there remains no reasonable likelihood that the marriage can be preserved.

9. During their _____-year marriage, and by reason of the marriage, the parties have accumulated a significant net worth, including, but not by way of limiting the generality of the foregoing: real property, investment accounts and retirement benefits, business and/or commercial real estate interests, and personalty, all of which requires equitable distribution by this Court.

10. The parties have enjoyed and become accustomed to an affluent standard of living, including substantial recreation, entertainment, travel, and other perquisites enjoyed only by successful business people in this community.

11. Defendant controls the parties' finances. Defendant routinely pays and/or provides money to Plaintiff to pay for (i) all mortgage payments, taxes, insurance premiums, maintenance expenses, and utility expenses associated with the parties' real properties, including the residence located at

Appendix

Sample Complaint for Divorce (Continued)

_____, (ii) travel and recreation expenses for the parties, (iii) all expenses of daily living, including but not limited to groceries, food, clothing expenses, unreimbursed medical and dental expenses, (iv) all expenses associated with the parties' vehicles (including but not limited to gasoline, maintenance, and insurance), (v) all credit card expenses/bills, and (vi) all health insurance. Defendant deposits her paychecks into the parties' joint checking account, which amounts to approximately $_____ per month, plus distributions and bonuses of an estimated $_____ per month, from which Plaintiff pays the household bills and the ordinary expenses of daily living for Plaintiff and the child(ren).

12.   Since Plaintiff has decided to begin divorce proceedings and the facts hereinafter set forth, he likewise is apprehensive that immediate and irreparable injury, loss or damage will result to him from the delay required to effect notice to Defendant or from the risk that notice will itself precipitate adverse action before an Order can be issued. Plaintiff's apprehension is based upon the fact that Defendant has full control, access to and knowledge of the parties' financial affairs and assets, thereby making it a simple matter for Defendant to dispose of or remove or secrete assets of the parties should she so choose. The parties' primary source of income is from Defendant's employment and Defendant's paychecks currently are deposited into the parties' joint account, from which Plaintiff pays the parties' household bills and daily living expenses. Plaintiff is fearful that Defendant will redirect her income into her own account thereby limiting his access to funds for living expenses for him and the child(ren).

13.   Based upon the foregoing, Plaintiff is justly fearful that unless protected by ex-parte injunctive orders of this Court, upon learning of the commencement of these proceedings, Defendant likely will or might:

a.   Surrender, borrow upon, use as collateral security, withdraw the cash surrender value of, assign, modify, transfer, change the beneficiary or beneficiaries of, or otherwise alter or cause any change to be made in any policy of life insurance which she owns or controls (individually or as Trustee) or in which she has any rights or interests, (legal or equitable), as owner, beneficiary, insured or otherwise;

b.   Surrender, redeem, cash in, withdraw, assign, modify, transfer, or encumber her interest in any pension, retirement, profit sharing, bonus, savings or stock purchase program in which she has any interest or, change the beneficiary or beneficiaries of said programs or of any other benefit payable by reason of her employment in the event of her death, disability, retirement or termination;

c.   Conceal, secrete, sell, assign, transfer (including transfers to herself or to any other person as Trustees, Guardian or Nominee), convey, mortgage or otherwise dispose of or encumber any of her assets (real or

191

Sample Complaint for Divorce (Continued)

personal, tangible or intangible), or any interest therein (legal or equitable), including but not limited to: stocks, bonds, or other securities, cash, checking accounts, savings accounts, automobiles, valuables contained in safe deposit boxes, or any other assets or business interests;

    d.   Destroy, damage, remove, or cause the removal of all or any part of the household furniture, furnishings, objects of art or equipment from the real properties of the parties;

    e.   Make purchases with cash, checks, or credit cards issued in the name of either or both parties, except to provide for the family's reasonable routine, ordinary, and necessary living expenses, consistent with the parties' past practices;

    f.   Take any action or fail to take any action so as to adversely affect the payment or maintenance in the ordinary course of any family expenses and/or household bills, including but not limited to, all of the federal, state and local income taxes of the parties; all real estate taxes of the parties in connection with real property owned by the parties; all mortgage payments, insurance payments, utilities payments, and general maintenance in connection with the real property owned by the parties, all credit card debts of the parties; all health insurance premiums and all uninsured health care expenses of the parties; all automobile expenses of the parties, including gasoline, insurance, registration, and routine maintenance; and all other accounts/liabilities of the parties; and

    g.   Redirect the deposit of funds/monies in a manner different from the pattern existing during the marriage; any or all of the above which conduct on the part of Defendant will hinder, obstruct, or make ineffectual this Court's jurisdiction and duty to make an equitable division and assignment of the assets of the parties.

    WHEREFORE, Plaintiff respectfully requests that:

A.   Plaintiff be awarded a Judgment of Divorce in accordance with the statutes in such cases made and provided;

B.   In accordance with the best interests of the parties' minor child(ren), the parties share joint legal custody, and Plaintiff be awarded physical custody of the parties' minor child(ren), with reasonable parenting time to Defendant;

C.   An appropriate amount of child support be determined in an accordance with the Michigan Child Support Guidelines;

D.   Defendant be required to provide reasonable sums for the support and maintenance of Plaintiff, the parties' minor child(ren), and the marital residence, temporarily during the pendency of this matter and permanently upon its conclusion, in the manner and style to which the parties have become accustomed;

Appendix

Sample Complaint for Divorce (Continued)

E.   This Court, through its provisions for discovery, compel Defendant to make a full and complete disclosure under oath of all assets of the parties, and that Plaintiff be awarded an equitable share of said assets by way of property settlement;

F.   This Court enter its *Ex Parte* Order for Preservation of Family Financial *Status Quo*;

G.   This Court enter its *Ex Parte* Mutual Asset Injunction;

H.   This Court award to Plaintiff such sums of money as shall be sufficient to provide permanent support for Plaintiff in the manner and style to which the parties have become accustomed;

I.   Defendant be required to pay such sums, both during the pendency of this action and at its conclusion, as are sufficient to adequately compensate Plaintiff's attorneys for representing Plaintiff in this action and to pay such expenses and other costs incurred by Plaintiff's attorneys in the protection of Plaintiff's interests; and

J.   Plaintiff may have such other and further relief in the premises as may be agreeable to equity and good conscience.

"I declare that the foregoing statements are true to the best of my information, knowledge and belief."

_____

_____, Plaintiff

Sample *Ex Parte* Mutual Asset Injunction

STATE OF MICHIGAN
IN THE CIRCUIT COURT FOR THE COUNTY OF_____.

	)	
_____	)	
Plaintiff,	)	
	)	
vs.	)	**Case No.**
	)	**HON.**
_____	)	_____
Defendant.	)	

EX PARTE MUTUAL
ASSET INJUNCTION

A session of said Court held in the City of_____, County of_____, State of Michigan, on_____.
PRESENT:

_____
CIRCUIT COURT JUDGE

Upon reading the verified *Complaint for Divorce and Petition for Ex Parte Relief of Plaintiff* herein, and it appearing that immediate and irreparable injury, loss, and damage will result to Plaintiff unless this Ex-Parte Mutual Asset Injunction is issued without notice to the Defendant, and the Court being fully advised in the premises;

NOW, THEREFORE, upon Motion of _____ of, attorneys for Plaintiff, _____,

IT IS HEREBY ORDERED that Defendant, _____, whose Social Security number is **xxx-xx-xxxx,** her agents, servants, employees and attorneys; Plaintiff, _____ whose Social Security number is **xxx-xx-xxxx,** his agents, servants, employees and attorneys; and those persons in active concert or participation with the parties shall not:

a.   Conceal, sell, assign, transfer (including transfers to themselves or to any other person as Trustees, Guardian or Nominee), convey, secrete, change the form of, encumber, mortgage, render illiquid, borrow against, withdraw from, or otherwise dispose of any of the parties' assets (whether real or personal, tangible or intangible), or any interest in those assets (whether legal or equitable), including but not limited to: real estate, business interests, investment holdings, stocks, bonds, or other securities; cash, checking

Sample Ex Parte Mutual Asset Injunction (Continued)

accounts, and savings accounts; automobiles, valuables contained in safe deposit boxes, or any other assets or business interests;

   b.   Surrender, borrow upon or against, use as collateral security, withdraw the cash surrender value of, assign, modify, transfer, change the beneficiary or beneficiaries of, or otherwise alter or cause any change to be made in any policy of life insurance which he/she owns or controls (individually or as Trustee) or in which he/she has any rights or interests, (legal or equitable), as owner, beneficiary, insured or otherwise;

   c.   Surrender, redeem, cash in, withdraw, assign, modify, transfer, or encumber his/her interest in any pension, retirement, profit sharing, bonus, savings or stock purchase program in which he/she has any interest or, change the beneficiary or beneficiaries of said programs or of any other benefit payable by reason of his/her employment in the event of his/her death, disability, retirement or termination; or

   d.   Destroy, damage, remove, or cause the removal of all or any part of the household furniture, furnishings, objects of art or equipment from the real properties of the parties;

   e.   Make purchases with cash, checks, or credit cards issued in the name of either or both parties, except to provide for the family's reasonable routine, ordinary, and necessary living expenses, consistent with the parties' past practices;

   f.   Take any action or fail to take any action so as to adversely affect the payment or maintenance in the ordinary course of any family expenses and/or household bills, including but not limited to, all of the federal, state and local income taxes of the parties; all real estate taxes of the parties in connection with real property owned by the parties; all mortgage payments, insurance payments, utilities payments, and general maintenance in connection with the real property owned by the parties, all credit card debts of the parties; all health insurance premiums and all uninsured health care expenses of the parties; all automobile expenses of the parties, including gasoline, insurance, registration, and routine maintenance; and all other accounts/liabilities of the parties; and

   g.   Redirect the deposit of funds/monies in a manner different from the pattern existing during the marriage.

   This *Ex Parte* Order will automatically become a temporary order unless a written objection or motion to modify or rescind this order and a request for a hearing is filed within fourteen (14) days of the date of service of this order.

Sample Ex Parte Mutual Asset Injunction (Continued)

NOTICE

1.   You may file a written objection to this order or a motion to modify or rescind this order. You must file the written objection or motion with the clerk of the court within 14 days after you were served with this order. You must serve a true copy of the objection or motion on the friend of the court and the party who obtained the order.

2.   If you file a written objection, the friend of the court must try to resolve the dispute. If the friend of the court cannot resolve the dispute and if you wish to bring this matter before the court without the assistance of counsel, the friend of the court must provide you with form pleadings and written instructions and must schedule a hearing with the court.

3.   The *ex parte* order will automatically become a temporary order if you do not file a written objection or motion to modify or rescind the *ex parte* order and a request for a hearing. Even if an objection is filed, the *ex parte* order will remain in effect and must be obeyed unless changed by a later court order.

_____

CIRCUIT COURT JUDGE

Drafted By:

Appendix

Sample *Ex Parte* Order for
Preservation of Family Financial *Status Quo*
STATE OF MICHIGAN
IN THE CIRCUIT COURT FOR THE COUNTY OF_____.

_____ **Plaintiff,**	)))
vs.	) **Case No.**) **HON.**)
_____ **Defendant.**	)) _____

EX PARTE ORDER FOR
PRESERVATION OF FAMILY FINANCIAL *STATUS QUO*

A a session of said Court held in the City of_____, County of_____, State of Michigan, on_____.
PRESENT:

_____
CIRCUIT COURT JUDGE

Upon reading the verified *Complaint for Divorce and Petition for Ex Parte Relief of Plaintiff* herein, and the Court being fully advised in the premises;

IT IS HEREBY ORDERED that the parties shall maintain the existing *status quo* of the parties by continuing to deposit in full any and all income received by either party into the parties' joint checking account, and from that account and/or other accounts customarily used by the parties, Defendant shall continue to pay in full the following:

i)   All of the federal, state and local income taxes of the parties;

ii)   All real estate taxes of the parties in connection with real property owned by the parties;

iii)   All mortgage payments, insurance payments, utilities payments, and general maintenance in connection with the real property owned by the parties;

iv)   All of the parties' routine, ordinary, and necessary credit card bills;

v)   All health insurance premiums and all unreimbursed health care expenses of the parties;

vi)   All automobile expenses of the parties, including gasoline, insurance, registration, and routine maintenance; and

vii)   All other reasonable and ordinary living expenses of the parties, consistent with the parties' past practices.

Sample *Ex Parte* Order for
Preservation of Family Financial *Status Quo* (Continued)

NOTICE

1.   You may file a written objection to this order or a motion to modify or rescind this order. You must file the written objection or motion with the clerk of the court within 14 days after you were served with this order. You must serve a true copy of the objection or motion on the friend of the court and the party who obtained the order.

2.   If you file a written objection, the friend of the court must try to resolve the dispute. If the friend of the court cannot resolve the dispute and if you wish to bring this matter before the court without the assistance of counsel, the friend of the court must provide you with form pleadings and written instructions and must schedule a hearing with the court.

3.   The *ex parte* order will automatically become a temporary order if you do not file a written objection or motion to modify or rescind the *ex parte* order and a request for a hearing. Even if an objection is filed, the *ex parte* order will remain in effect and must be obeyed unless changed by a later court order.

_____

CIRCUIT COURT JUDGE

Drafted By:

Resources

Annual Credit Report Request Service
www.annualcreditreport.com
P.O. Box 105283
Atlanta, GA 30348-5283
(877) 322–8228

This website offers a centralized service for consumers to request annual credit reports. It was created by the three nationwide consumer credit reporting companies: Equifax, Experian, and Trans Union. AnnualCreditReport.com processes requests for free credit file disclosures (commonly called credit reports). Under the *Fair and Accurate Credit Transactions Act (FACT Act),* consumers can request and obtain a free credit report once every twelve months from each of the three nationwide consumer credit reporting companies. AnnualCreditReport.com offers consumers a fast and convenient way to request, view, and print their credit reports in a secure Internet environment. It also provides options to request reports by telephone and by mail.

American Academy of Matrimonial Lawyers
www.aaml.org
150 North Michigan Avenue, Suite 1420
Chicago, Illinois 60601
(312) 263-7477

Founded in 1962, the attorneys admitted to the American Academy of Matrimonial Lawyers are recognized as highly skilled negotiators and litigators who represent individuals in all facets of family law. These areas include divorce, annulment, prenuptial agreements, postnuptial agreements, marital settlement agreements, child custody and visitation, business valuations, property valuations and division, alimony, child support, and other family law issues.

Best Lawyers

www.bestlawyers.com
New York Office
45 Main Street, Suite 820
Brooklyn, New York 11201
(718) 509-6095
Best Lawyers is the oldest and most highly respected peer review guide to the legal profession worldwide. You can search the lists of peer-recommended lawyers by individual, firm, practice area, and location.

Detroit Free Legal Aid Clinic, Inc.

www.detroitflac.com
5425 Woodward Avenue
Detroit, Michigan 48202
(313) 883-0058
The Free Legal Aid Clinic provides legal assistance to low income and elderly residents of Wayne County in the areas of family law and elder law. The clinic focuses on assisting victims of domestic abuse and elder abuse. It is staffed entirely by Wayne State University Law School students who provide legal services under the supervision of licensed attorneys.

Friend of the Court/Michigan (FOC) Information

www.friendofthecourt.org
This website gives information regarding the Michigan Friend of the Court System, including the role of the Friend of the Court, services of Friend of the Court, and additional resources such as downloadable court forms, Michigan counties local information (including but not limited to Wayne, Macomb, and Oakland counties), and handbooks, Rights and Responsibilities of the Parties; Friend of the Court Duties; Procedure of the Courts; Alternate Dispute Resolution (ADR); Information about Custody, Parenting Time and Support; and Glossary of Frequently Used Terms.

Internal Revenue Service (IRS)

www.irs.gov
Phone: (800) 829-1040 tax assistance for individual tax questions or (800) 829-4933 for business tax questions. The IRS website allows you to search for any keyword, review publications and information on tax questions, or submit a question via e-mail or phone to an IRS representative.

Resources

Michigan Bar Association
www.michbar.org
State Bar of Michigan
306 Townsend Street
Lansing, Michigan 48933-2012
(517) 346-6300
(800) 968-1442

This website includes a Find Legal Assistance page to find an attorney, as well as a Family Law page that gives an introduction to family law topics, Michigan statutes, legal forms, and Michigan guides, which includes publications prepared by the Legislative Council. General interest publications include Friend of the Court: Support Custody and Visitation for Michigan Children and Domestic Violence and your Child: A Parent's Guide to Health and Safety.

Michigan Coalition to End
Domestic and Sexual Violence (MCEDSV)
www.mcedsv.org
3893 Okemos Road, Suite B2
Okemos, Michigan 48864-4209
(517) 347-7000

The MCEDSV is dedicated to the empowerment of all the state's survivors of domestic and sexual violence. Their mission is to develop and promote efforts aimed at the elimination of all domestic and sexual violence in Michigan by supporting and building upon the services provided by the network of local programs.

Michigan Department of Health and Human Services
http://michigan.gov/dhs
Michigan Department of Human Services
235 South Grand Avenue
P.O. Box 30037
Lansing, Michigan 48009
Child Support: (866) 540-0008
General Information: (855) ASK-MICH

The Michigan Department of Health and Human Services is built to promote better health outcomes, reduce health risks, and support stable and safe families while encouraging self-sufficiency. The website has information regarding abuse and neglect, children's protective services; domestic violence, and child support.

Michigan Legal Help

http://michiganlegalhelp.org

The Michigan Legal Help website was created to help people who have simple legal problems without a lawyer. There are articles to assist individuals to learn about a specific area of the law and toolkits to help prepare oneself. The Michigan Legal Help website does not provide legal advice and is not a substitute for having a lawyer.

Social Security Administration

www.ssa.gov
Office of Public Inquiries
Windsor Park Building
6401 Security Blvd. Baltimore, MD 21235
(800) 772-1213

The website enables users to search for a question or word, submit questions via e-mail, or review recent publications.

Super Lawyers

http://superlawyers.com

Super Lawyers is a rating service of outstanding lawyers from more than seventy practice areas who have attained a high-degree of peer recognition and professional achievement. The selection process includes independent research, peer nominations, and peer evaluations.

Other Recommendations:

National Domestic Violence Hotline

(800) 799-SAFE (7223)

Glossary

Affidavit: A written statement of facts made under oath and signed before a notary public. Affidavits are used primarily when there will not be a hearing in open court with live testimony. The attorney will prepare an affidavit to present relevant facts. Affidavits may be signed by the parties or in some cases by witnesses. The person signing the affidavit may be referred to as the *affiant*.

Alimony: Court-ordered spousal support payments from one party to another, often to enable the recipient spouse to become economically independent.

Allegation: A statement that one party claims is true.

Answer: A written response to the petition for divorce. It serves to admit or deny the allegations in the complaint and may also make claims against the opposing party. This is sometimes called a *responsive pleading*. An answer should be filed within thirty days of either (a) the complaint being served by the sheriff or (b) the defendant's voluntary appearance being filed with the court.

Appeal: The process by which a higher court reviews the decision of a lower court. In Michigan family law cases, a person will first file an appeal with the Michigan Court of Appeals. After that appeal is decided, there may be a further appeal to the Michigan Supreme Court.

Application for removal of jurisdiction: A parent's written request to the court seeking permission to relocate to another state with the children.

Application to modify: A party's written request to the court to change a prior order regarding custody, child support, alimony, or any other order that the court may change by law.

Child support: Financial support for a child paid by the noncustodial parent to the custodial parent.

Complaint: The first document filed with the clerk of the court in an action for divorce, separation, or paternity. The complaint sets forth the facts on which the requested relief is based.

Contempt of court: The willful and intentional failure of a party to comply with a court order, judgment, or decree. Contempt may be punishable by a fine or jail.

Contested case: Any case in which the parties cannot reach an agreement. A contested case will result in a trial to have the judge decide disputed issues.

Court order: A court-issued document setting forth the judge's orders. An order can be issued based upon the parties' agreement or the judge's decision. An order may require the parties to perform certain acts or set forth their rights and responsibilities. An order is put in writing, signed by the judge, and filed with the court.

Court order acceptable for processing (COAP): A type of court order that provides for payment of civil service retirement to a former spouse.

Cross-examination: The questioning of a witness by the opposing counsel during trial or at a deposition, in response to questions asked by the other lawyer.

Custody: The legal right and responsibility awarded by a court for the possession of, care of, and decision making for a minor child.

Decree of dissolution: A final court order dissolving the marriage, dividing property and debts, ordering support, and entering other orders regarding finances and the minor children.

Defendant: The responding party to a divorce; the party who did not file the complaint initiating the divorce.

Deposition: A witness's testimony taken out of court, under oath, and in the presence of lawyers and a court reporter. If a person gives a different testimony at the time of trial, he or she can be impeached with the deposition testimony; that is, statements made at a deposition can be used to show untruthfulness if a different answer is given at trial.

Glossary

Direct examination: The initial questioning of a witness in court by the lawyer who called him or her to the stand.

Discovery: A process used by attorneys to discover information from the opposing party for the purpose of fully assessing a case for settlement or trial. Types of discovery include interrogatories, requests for production of documents, and requests for admissions.

Dissolution: The act of terminating or dissolving a marriage.

Equitable distribution of property: The method by which real and personal property and debts are divided in a divorce. Given all economic circumstances of the parties, Michigan law requires that marital property and debts be divided in a fair and reasonable manner.

Ex parte: Usually in reference to a motion, the term used to describe an appearance of only one party before the judge, without the other party being present. For example, an *ex parte* restraining order may be granted immediately after the filing of a complaint for divorce.

Guardian *ad litem* (GAL): A person, often a lawyer or mental health professional, appointed by a court to conduct an investigation regarding the children's best interests.

Hearing: Any proceeding before the court for the purpose of resolving disputed issues between the parties through presentation of testimony, affidavits, exhibits, or argument.

Hold-harmless clause: A term in a court order that requires one party to assume responsibility for a debt and to protect the other spouse from any loss or expense in connection with it, as in to "hold harmless from liability."

Interrogatories: Written questions sent from one party to the other that are used to obtain facts or opinions related to the divorce.

Joint custody: The shared right and responsibility of both parents awarded by the court for possession, care, and decision making for children.

Mediation: A process by which a neutral third party facilitates negotiations between the parties on a wide range of issues.

Motion: A written application to the court for relief, such as temporary child support, custody, or restraining orders.

No-fault divorce: The type of divorce Michigan has that does not require evidence of marital misconduct. This means that abandonment, cruelty, and adultery are neither relevant nor required to be proven for the purposes of granting the divorce.

Notice of hearing: A written statement sent to the opposing lawyer or spouse listing the date and place of a hearing and the nature of the matters that will be heard by the court. In Michigan, one party is required to give the other party reasonable notice of any court hearing.

Party: The person in a legal action whose rights or interests will be affected by the divorce. For example, in a divorce the parties include the wife and husband.

Pending: During the case. For example, the judge may award you temporary support while your case is pending.

Petitioner: A term formerly used to refer to the plaintiff or person who files the complaint seeking a divorce.

Plaintiff: The person who files the complaint initiating a divorce.

Pleadings: Documents filed with the court seeking a court order.

Qualified domestic relations order (QDRO): A type of court order that provides for direct payment from a retirement account to a former spouse.

Qualified medical support order (QMSO): A type of court order that provides a former spouse certain rights regarding medical insurance and information.

Request for production of documents: A written request for documents sent from one party to the other during the discovery process.

Sequester: To order prospective witnesses out of the courtroom until they have concluded giving their testimony.

Set off: A debt or financial obligation of one spouse that is deducted from the debt or financial obligation of the other spouse.

Settlement: The agreed resolution of disputed issues.

Show cause: Written application to the court to hold another person in contempt of court for violating or failing to comply with a current court order.

Stipulation: An agreement reached between parties or an agreement by their attorneys.

Subpoena: A document delivered to a person or witness that requires him or her to appear in court, appear for a deposition, or produce documents. Failure to comply could result in punishment by the court. A subpoena requesting documents is called a subpoena *duces tecum*.

Temporary restraining order (TRO): An order of the court prohibiting a party from certain behavior. For example, a temporary restraining order may order a person not to transfer any funds during a pending divorce action.

Trial: A formal court hearing in which the judge will decide disputed issues raised by the parties' pleadings.

Under advisement: A term used to describe the status of a case, usually after a court hearing on a motion or a trial, when the judge has not yet made a decision.

Index

Index

Index

with attorney, 24, 33, 40–41

during mediation, 70

with spouse, 102–103

community property, 130

compassion, 24

complaint for divorce, 9, *see also* divorce complaint

acknowledgment of service and agreement for, 10

sample, 189–193

confidentiality, 20, 33–34, 55

Consolidated Omnibus Budget Reconciliation Act (COBRA), 149

contempt of court, 118

contingency fee, 45

coping with divorce, 21, *see also* stress

cost-of-living allowance (COLA), 152

costs, *see* attorney fees; fees

county requirements, 7

court, *see also* trial

adjournments of court dates for, 173

child/children present in, 89–90

court clerk's role in, 175

court reporter's role in, 175–176

courtroom etiquette in, 175

dates for, 171

emotional breakdown during, 26–27

frequency of going to, 171–172

going to, 170–182

Indian tribal, 7–8

jury in, 173

notice for appearing in, 172

personal support during, 180

property settlement agreement and, going to, 146

questions asked by attorney during, 176–177

required attendance to, 172

settlement agreement and going to, 174

spouse's attendance to, 172, 180

status conference in, 173

talking to attorney during, 176

for temporary hearing, 174

testifying in, 173

court clerk, 175

court dates, adjournments of, 173

court hearings, *see* hearing

Court of Appeals, 36

court orders, *see* order

court reporter, 175–176

courtroom etiquette, 175

Court Rules, 58

credit cards, 156–158

cross-examination, 181–182

D

date of valuation, 140–141

dates for court, 171

dating, 91

death

alimony and, 127

child custody and, 107

pension and, 152

property and, division of, 147

retirement and, 152

Social Security and, 152

debt, *see also* debts, division of

accrual of, during divorce process, 158

marital, 130

premarital, 158

property and determining, division of, 145

debts, division of, 155–161

bankruptcy and, 159–161

credit cards, 156–158

debt accrual during divorce process, 158

during divorce process, 156

213

Index

Friend of the Court (FOC), 55,
  108, 112, 114, 116–118
friends, *see* personal support
furniture, 135

G

gay, 92
general everyday expenses,
  119
get cooperation clause, 145
gifts, 139–140
Gmail, 34
grounds for divorce, 4–5
guardian *ad litem* (GAL),
  35–36, 48
  appointing, 73
  child custody, role in deter-
    mining, 95
  fees for, 48

H

harm to child/children, reducing risk of, 70
head of household tax status,
  165
health insurance, 119, 148–
  149
health savings account (HSA),
  141
hearing, 10, *see also* temporary
  hearing
heterosexuality, 92
hidden assets, 134–135, 143
hold-harmless clause, 158–
  159
home/house, 130–134, *see*
  also mortgage
  equity in, 132–133
  exclusive possession of,
    during divorce process, 81
  factors in determining pos-
    session of, 130
  household goods in, posses-
    sion of, 134
  payments on, 156
  property, division of, 130–
    134
  selling of, during divorce
    process, 131
  taxes, sale of, 166

valuation of, 131–132
homosexuality, 92
hourly rates for attorney fees,
  45–46
household goods, 134

I

immigration status, 7
in camera meeting, 86
income equalization, 126
income rental, 112
income taxes, 162–163
Income Withholding Order,
  114
Indian tribal court, 7–8
indigency, 48
infidelity, 5, 90, 124
information, *see also* documentation
  alimony, provided to attor-
    ney about, 123
  attorney, gathering for, 22
  deadlines for gathering, 22
  from employer, 60
  financial, 16, 60
  for initial consultation, 31
  subpoena for, 60
  timely responses to requests
    for, 53
inheritances, 138–140
initial consultation
  attorney fees for, 44
  expectations during, 32–33
  information for, 31
  law language used during,
    32
  personal support during,
    34
innocent spouse relief, 169
instate residential requirements, 5
insurance, 119, 148–149, 153
interest from certificates of
  deposit, 141
Internal Revenue Service
  (IRS)
  alimony, considerations of,
    163
  Form 8332 (Release/Revoca-

Index

Index

About the Author

John F. Schaefer has practiced law continuously since 1969, and is the founder of The Law Firm of John F. Schaefer, with offices in Birmingham and Grosse Pointe, Michigan. He specializes in complex matrimonial matters and has been an adjunct professor at the Detroit College of Law (now Michigan State University College of Law), teaching courses in domestic relations for more than thirty years. Mr. Schaefer attended Cranbrook School, the University of Notre Dame, Michigan State University, and the Detroit College of Law. He earned bachelor of arts and Juris Doctor degrees and he also holds an honorary doctor of laws degree.

Mr. Schaefer's expertise, reputation, and experience have been recognized by, and he is listed in *The Best Lawyers in America* (first edition and all subsequent editions) and *Who's Who in America,* among other publications. Mr. Schaefer is and has been associated with numerous organizations and has served them variously, including: American Academy of Matrimonial Lawyers (past president, Michigan chapter); Detroit College of Law Foundation (chairman); Detroit College of Law (trustee 1986 to 2001); Michigan State University College of Law (trustee emeritus 2001 to date); Michigan State Bar Foundation (fellow); Oakland County Bar Association (past president); State Bar of Michigan: Family Law Section (past chairman); Attorney Grievance Commission (arbitrator); Committee on Character and Fitness; Beaumont Hospitals (trustee); and The Detroit Police Athletic League (former director).

Mr. Schaefer has instructed hundreds of Michigan circuit court judges and thousands of practicing lawyers in the substantive law of matrimonial matters through the Michigan Judicial Institute and the Institute of Continuing Legal Education (ICLE). Mr. Schaefer is the author of *Family Law in Michigan,* a publication of ICLE, and he has written numerous articles and made numerous television and radio appearances relative to legal matters. In 2010, Michigan State University College of

Law dedicated and named the law library "The John F. Schaefer Law Library" and dedicated The John F. Schaefer Chair in Matrimonial Law. *The Best Lawyers in America* named John F. Schaefer Lawyer of the Year for 2013 for family law in the metropolitan Detroit area.

In furtherance of his courtroom accomplishments, among Mr. Schaefer's many notable cases include *Dart v. Dart,* a case involving the laws and courts of England and assets in excess of $1 billion; *Nasser v. Nasser,* representing the 36-year wife of Jacques Nasser, the then-CEO of Ford Motor Company; and two cases of *Iacocca v. Iacocca,* representing two of the wives of Lee Iacocca, the former CEO of Chrysler Corporation. He has also represented the distinguished and preeminent Robert A. Lutz, former president of Chrysler Corporation and vice chairman of General Motors Corporation.

THE LAW FIRM OF

JOHN F. SCHAEFER

380 North Old Woodard Ave., Ste. 320
Birmingham, MI 48009
(248) 642-6655

130 Kercheval
Grosse Point Farms, MI 48236
(313) 881-1300
www.lfjfs.com

Divorce Titles from Addicus Books

Visit our online catalog at www.AddicusBooks.com

Divorce in Alabama: The Legal Process, Your Rights, and What to Expect $21.95

Divorce in Arizona: The Legal Process, Your Rights, and What to Expect. $21.95

Divorce in California: The Legal Process, Your Rights, and What to Expect $21.95

Divorce in Connecticut: The Legal Process, Your Rights, and What to Expect $21.95

Divorce in Florida: The Legal Process, Your Rights, and What to Expect $21.95

Divorce in Georgia: Simple Answers to Your Legal Questions $21.95

Divorce in Hawaii: The Legal Process, Your Rights, and What to Expect $21.95

Divorce in Illinois: The Legal Process, Your Rights, and What to Expect $21.95

Divorce in Louisiana: The Legal Process, Your Rights, and What to Expect $21.95

Divorce in Maine: The Legal Process, Your Rights, and What to Expect $21.95

Divorce in Michigan: The Legal Process, Your Rights, and What to Expect. $21.95

Divorce in Mississippi: The Legal Process, Your Rights, and What to Expect. $21.95

Divorce in Missouri: The Legal Process, Your Rights, and What to Expect $21.95

Divorce in Nebraska: The Legal Process, Your Rights, and What to Expect—2nd Edition $21.95

Divorce in Nevada: The Legal Process, Your Rights, and What to Expect. $21.95

Divorce in New Jersey: The Legal Process, Your Rights, and What to Expect $21.95

Divorce in New York: The Legal Process, Your Rights, and What to Expect $21.95

Divorce in North Carolina: The Legal Process, Your Rights, and What to Expect $21.95

Divorce in Tennessee: The Legal Process, Your Rights, and What to Expect $21.95

Divorce in Virginia: The Legal Process, Your Rights, and What to Expect $21.95

Divorce in Washington: The Legal Process, Your Rights, and What to Expect $21.95

Divorce in West Virginia: The Legal Process, Your Rights, and What to Expect $21.95

Divorce in Wisconsin: The Legal Process, Your Rights, and What to Expect $21.95

To Order Books:

Visit us online at: www.AddicusBooks.com
Call toll free: (800) 888-4741

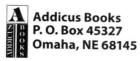

Addicus Books
P. O. Box 45327
Omaha, NE 68145